Fishermen and Merchants in 19th Century Gaspé

The Fishermen–Dealers of William Hyman and Sons

Roch Samson

Studies in Archaeology
Architecture and History

National Historic Parks and Sites Branch
Parks Canada
Environment Canada
1984

"*You know, in spring nobody had a cent. Me, I had no money, so I went to Grande-Grave, got my fishing gear, got stuff for the family, I had an account there, right. Well, comes around August 15, if I had enough to pay my account, well I gave what I had on it, then I finished in the fall. Then if I had ten dollars or around there, well I had a good summer. You know, we didn't count money in the hundreds or even in the fifties, no, no, no, when a man finished his summer, if he could clear twenty-five bucks, dammit, he was rich!...*" (translation)

"*...even if you were in debt, they gave you credit all the same, just to keep you there....*" (translation)

"*...their aim, them people that time there, was to keep the poor man down, and it's only the ones who would have some education who would ever come out of the hole. The ones who had no education, it didn't matter they were French, English, they had them there, they kept them there. Suppose they make a big summer there, they never got a cent, they put it there and the next year, if it was a poor year, they kept it....*"

Statements from fishermen who lived through the merchant credit system in the early 20th century in Gaspé Bay, gathered by the author in 1976.

Fishermen and Merchants in 19th Century Gaspé
The Fishermen-Dealers of William Hyman and Sons

Roch Samson

Submitted for publication in 1981 by Roch Samson, Quebec Region, Parks Canada.

ACKNOWLEDGEMENTS

This study was made possible by Percival Gerald Hyman who bequeathed to Parks Canada the William Hyman and Sons Company archives, and by David Hyman, Percival's son, who allowed us access to the company's correspondence. Our research on the land transactions in the Forillon area was facilitated by Owen Bouchard and Jean Bourget, registry officer and protonotary of the district of Gaspé at the Percé Court House, respectively. Thérèse Savoie, anthropologist, helped update and compile the data and participated in the research on the history of the Forillon fishing establishments. Yvan Breton and François Trudel, anthropologists at Laval University, helped determine the approach of the study. Thanks also to André Lepage, anthropologist, for such fruitful discussions. Finally, sincere thanks to François Pellerin who prepared the drawings.

INTRODUCTION

This study is part of the work done in connection with the restoration of the old fishing establishment at Grande-Grave, which is now in Forillon National Park. Its contents should help in the historical interpretation of the social and economic life of merchants and fishermen who lived in Forillon. The archives of William Hyman and Sons (1845-1967) formed most of the documentary basis for the work. The ledgers and part of the company correspondence have been systematically examined to reconstitute and analyze the production relations that bound the Hyman company and the fishermen together. Quebec historiographers have seldom used this archival material until now, and it has disclosed a wealth of extraordinary information about the activities of a population. The guiding principle for the work was economic anthropology, and its purpose to show how Gaspé society was shaped by the manner in which the production of dried cod was organized. Gaspé was settled and populated through a systematic exploitation of cod, so that a study of this process constitutes a most valuable means of access to its history.

Dependent Fishermen and Monopolistic Merchants

The general purpose of this study is to describe the business structure and the organization of Gaspé fisheries in the 19th century. More specifically, it will analyze the social and economic conditions of fishermen in their relations with merchant exporters of dried cod.[1] The records made it possible on the one hand to reconstruct the activities of a Gaspé merchant in his relations with his fishermen-dealers over a ten-year period (1854-63), and on the other to see how this merchant fit into a business system that was dominated by Channel Islands' companies. From observation and analysis of the trade practices of William Hyman, an attempt will be made to show how these practices were part of a much broader business structure. At the same time as the operations of this system are being described, it will be shown how this business system contributed towards making Gaspé fishermen dependent on merchants.

The historiographical contribution of this study updates what is known of the economic mechanisms that contributed throughout the 19th century to the Gaspé fishermen's dependency on merchants representing Channel Islands' capital in Gaspé. It is within the framework of this dependency that the technical and social conditions for the production of dried cod, called the production process, will be investigated in terms of how they related to the region's methods of supply and its methods of disposing of its products under the monopoly control of the merchants, called the circulation process. After these processes or mechanisms have been described, it will be shown how the indebtedness of fishermen, which was a condition of their dependency, was an essential feature for the viability of the commercial fisheries exploitation system.

Gaspé Historiography: A Critical View

From the beginning of the 19th century, the trade system set up by Channel Islands' merchants after 1760 was sufficiently well established to be called a monopoly. Members of the clergy were the first to denounce the system, which caused the fishermen to go into debt and to become dependent. They also deplored the lack of agricultural development and the absence of schools. In 1821 Doctor von Iffland, sent to Gaspé to vaccinate the residents against smallpox, became aware of a similar problem. He visited the area at the time the Taschereau Commission was about to give land grants in the hope of encouraging agriculture. Doctor von Iffland saw clearly the danger inherent in such a policy, which would result in building a merchant monopoly over the land and the beaches. In effect the fishermen's debts to the merchants would, he felt, make it possible for the merchants to expropriate over two-thirds of the land in the district. The power held by the merchants as a result of a system of advances and credit was therefore a major impediment to agricultural development. The agricultural illusion nevertheless continued through to the end of the century.

Beginning in 1852, the fisheries inspectors, who were of course well informed about the workings of the commercial system, prolonged the illusion, especially during the periods of scarcity following poor fishing seasons (chapter four). Moreover, except for the archives of the merchant companies, the reports of these inspectors are the best sources of data available on the organization of fishing and on conditions for fishermen. The annual inspectors' recommendations to diversify the fisheries and to encourage Canadian businessmen to become involved in this lucrative field were not supported by politicians whose decisions were usually governed by an agriculturalist ideology.

Thus instead of analyzing the organization of fisheries to make the changes needed, especially in the living conditions of fishermen, diversification of fisheries, the introduction of new methods, and foreign control over this economic sector, the replacement of fishing by agriculture as the principal activity was advocated. This of course was to misunderstand and underestimate the degree to which a tested commercial system was established, with much of the population specialized in producing dried cod, and to overestimate the agricultural potential of Gaspé. In general, fishing did not have a good image because of the way it forced fishermen to live in misery and also because the clergy did not like to see Catholics mingling with Protestant fishermen and merchants.

Finally, both the clergy and the politicians were well aware that Gaspé fishermen were caught in the workings of a "system" that established their dependence on the merchants. By encouraging agriculture, it was possible to avoid questioning the operating rules of the "system," whose very logic was an obstacle to the development of agriculture, because it forced agriculture to play strictly a subsistence role.

The commentaries that followed the disappearance of the Channel Islands' companies from Gaspé at the end of the 19th century reveal that analysis of the situation still had not progressed very far.[2] When the flow of Channel Islands' capital was suddenly interrupted because of crises affecting European capital from 1873 on, bankruptcies and closings of major companies left the Gaspé fisheries in a state of disarray because they had become so completely absorbed into the system.[3]

Attempting to interpret the significance of the demise of the system raised once again the problem of the exploitation of fishermen. From the point of view of former company officers, the companies failed because they gave too much credit to the fishermen, who allowed themselves to be supported in this way rather than pay their debts.[4] From the fishermen's standpoint, they were kept dependent and indebted to the companies' monopoly and were not given any opportunity to escape from it.[5]

At first glance it seems plausible from the companies' point of view that in a crisis, large extensions of credit in the form of advances to the fishermen may well have put the companies in a precarious position. From the fishermen's point of view, the ways of obtaining supplies, which soon led to debt and risks of expropriation, kept them from any kind of social fulfillment. The actors who lived out the drama of the credit system saw quite clearly the tensions and relationships that bound them together, but it was yet to be shown that these relationships were essential to maintaining production. The historian Harold A. Innis was the first to see social relations in the context of a large commercial structure precisely because of his main interest, which was to show that the fishing industry, by its very nature, developed on the basis of many isolated fishing ports over a wide area, as opposed to the centralization required by the fur trade. He was able to isolate the main factors underlying the maintenance and the eventual collapse of the merchant system on the Atlantic coast and the Gulf of St. Lawrence, and his analysis introduced several factors relating to the constraints that were part of the commercial structure of the fishing industry.[6]

On the one hand, Innis linked the growth of the use of credit (in the form of the truck, or barter system, from the French word "troc") to outside fluctuations which could not be controlled (incomes that fluctuated with the catch and the price of fish, market conditions and government intervention). On the other hand, he stated that the imbalance of international trade added to the internal burden put upon the truck system. The commercial organization provided a "crude insurance system" which balanced declines in one district against profits in another, losses in one season against gains in other seasons, and the losses suffered by some fishermen against the gains made by others. The credit system was seen as the best way, albeit cumbersome, of exploiting fishing resources in a viable manner.

Innis's perspective is useful insofar as he attempted to isolate the main components of the commercial structure of the fishing industry, and saw in the credit system the driving force that made it work. This

10

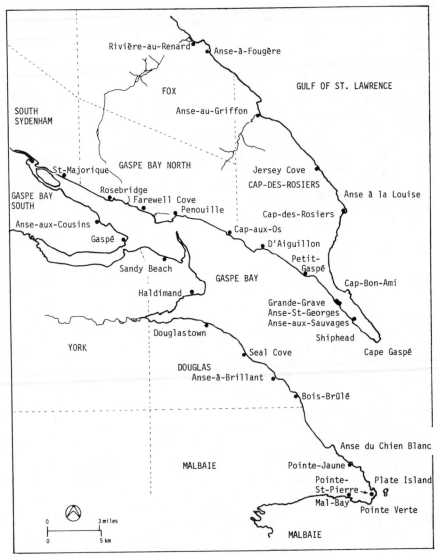

1. Forillon and Gaspé Bay in the mid-19th century.

study will take his analysis further by examining one merchant's day-to-day application of the credit system and how it fitted into the overall development of merchant capital in Gaspé.

Studies of Quebec's economic history by Ouellet[7] and Hamelin and Roby[8] have partly taken up Innis's point of view and attempted to explain the underdevelopment of Gaspé. They argue that the Gaspé mentality is imprisoned in custom and tradition. Traces of this short-sighted viewpoint have been seen in reports from the Eastern Quebec Planning Board in the mid-sixties, and it was largely from this point of view that the Quebec government undertook the retraining and reloca-tion of coastal fishermen in the seventies. We prefer another approach -- an examination of the daily life of 19th century fisherman through a study and analysis of their everyday dealings with the merchants. A systematic study of the dynamics of this relationship will, it is hoped, help to challenge the notion that Gaspé society was ultra-conservative, and permit a better understanding of its transition to another form of organization in the 20th century.

Chapter one of this study gives a brief history of how William Hyman and Sons became established in the Gaspé and the company's importance to the area. Chapters two and three are more detailed: they describe the production process for dried cod with an account of the constraints that governed cod production, and its technical and social aspects. Chapter four contains a quantitative and qualitative analysis of the dynamics of debt between the Hyman company and its fishermen-dealers. The conclusion returns to the original hypothesis and judges merchant capital as a means of development. Finally, Appendix I describes the theoretical orientation and defines the concepts of pro-duction process and circulation process, showing their pertinence in understanding the merchant system as it was reconstituted in 19th century Gaspesia.

Note: In this text the words "merchant" and "company" are used indifferently to refer to the economic agents who supplied advances to fishermen, bought and exported the dry cod. The owner of a fishing room hiring fishermen and dealing with the Hyman company is a "beach master," a "dealer" or a "planter." In one case "beach master" refers rather to the foreman of a company fishing establishment. The owner of a small establishment hiring only members of his family is called an "independent fisherman," but most of the time a "fisherman." Finally, the "individual fisherman" hired by a company or a dealer is refered to as "fisherman" or "employee."

I WILLIAM HYMAN AND SONS[1]

The Gaspé Merchant in the Mid-19th Century

When merchant William Hyman acquired his first fishing establish-ment at Grande-Grave in 1845, cod fishing and the cod industry were firmly established in the area. Following Charles Robin's initiative at Paspébiac in 1766, merchants and entrepreneurs from the Channel Islands were almost everywhere along the coast, which meant an increasing population of fishermen. Elsewhere we have described how entrepreneurs and fishermen first settled permanently in the Gaspé after the British conquest.[2] The main features of this settlement period are, first, the monopoly on the cod industry which Channel Islands' merchants quickly established at the end of the 18th century; second, the mer-chants' control over the fishing sites and the extreme mobility of fishermen; third, the fact that the work force was composed almost exclusively of seasonal fishermen from 1760 to 1800, working within merchants' or companies' large organizations. After 1800 this work force was recruited more and more from a resident population which had settled around many small establishments on the outskirts of large company establishments. The mobility of fishermen and entrepreneurs (independent producers) had its roots in the gradual advance of the Channel Islanders' monopoly. At the beginning of the 19th century the Robin company had the monopoly on Chaleur Bay trade, and the Janvrin company, which was also connected with Robin, controlled the Gaspé Bay. In 1820, almost thirty years after the Janvrin company had set up its establishment at Grande-Grave, the fishermen were so in debt that the company could have expropriated most of them.[3] The power of these companies was based on their total control of the circulation process: they owned the shipping fleets and the stores where fishermen had to buy their goods. Entrepreneurs who came to set up business in the Gaspé sooner or later had to contact these companies for financing and provisions, and so lost their autonomy.[4] It was only after 1830 that the arrival of John Le Boutillier, a former agent of the Robin company, presented any serious competition for them. He had already set up two outports (or stations) in Janvrin and Robin territory in 1836, one at Anse-au-Griffon and the other at Percé.[5] Around 1838 Le Boutillier set up two more at Paspébiac and Bonaventure Island.[6] Other companies sprang up around Chaleur Bay and Gaspé Bay, which made for stronger competition. In 1855 another Jersey man, William Fruing, also a former agent of the Robin company, acquired the Janvrin company at Grande-Grave, next door to the Hyman company.[7] The firms diversified and consolidated, but it was still a Channel Islands' monopoly, as were all supply and export operations. We'll see later that Hyman, who acquired a Channel Islands' business, also had to use this network for provisions and exports.

By the mid-19th century settlement by increasing the number of small fishing posts had brought about many new production sites. The large establishments, however, remained the most important production centres. Every summer French-Canadian workers and fishermen poured in mainly from the area around Montmagny. The Robin company had initiated this summer migration at the turn of the century[8] and it continued until around 1880. The Hyman company took in its share of Canadiens each season, but as we shall see, half of its production came from small local producers.[9] Merchants competed with each other in giving advances or credit to these producers, and undoubtedly this was how Hyman set up stiff competition to the Jersey companies.

History of the Company

Readers familiar with Anglo-Norman family names in the Gaspé will probably wonder how Hyman, originally a Russian Jew, came to be one of the leading merchants in the Gaspé cod-fishing industry. According to available accounts[10] he must have been enterprising but beyond that, we don't know how he got into the Gaspé merchant world. His correspondence leads us to believe he got financial backing from Donald Fraser, a Quebec broker, from his son Thomas, and from Abraham Joseph, an influential Jewish financier in Quebec City.[11] Again according to his correspondence, Hyman was already active in the Gaspé cod industry in 1842,[12] although the first legal document of his presence as a merchant dates from 1845. That was the year he acquired his first fishing establishment at Grande-Grave from Francis Ahier, a Guernsey merchant captain living at Anse-St-Georges.[13]

We have scant information on the first nine years of the company's operation from 1845 to 1853; the first ledgers in the archives date from 1854, probably because of a fire that destroyed the company office in the winter of 1855-56.[14] Records of Hyman's land transactions around Forillon, however, give us some indication of his business activities. From these we have been able to establish that because fishermen were always in debt, their real estate holdings were directly proportional to their economic status as dealers. Most of Hyman's real estate dealings were with his dealers, and were often a type of bond, sale or mortgage. Thérèse Savoie has compiled an interesting report on the land trans-actions of Hyman and Fruing, who were competing in the same territory.[15] Basing her analysis on the type of transactions and on the location of the lots traded, she shows us how bonds, mortgages, judicial decisions and the buying and reselling of property were the mainstays of the companies' real estate activity -- which paralleled their business activity based on credit. Appendix B provides some very interesting statistics on this subject.

According to T. Savoie, the Hyman company's early years saw a series of purchases of land lots, mostly around Gaspé Bay and Cap-des-Rosiers. This was the period of establishment and consolidation of the company in terms of investments. Legal actions came later in the 1860s. Compared with the Fruing company, whose operations took place over a larger territory, Hyman had a greater concentration of activity around

2. William Hyman. (A.D. Hart, ed., *The Jew in Canada* ..., Jewish Publications Ltd., 1926)

Grande-Grave during the eighty years studied by T. Savoie.16
     By 1860 nearly every family on the Forillon peninsula had an account with William Hyman and Sons. As the number of Hyman dealers grew, Hyman increased the number of his fishing ports, stores and

warehouses, until at his death in 1882 he owned two fishing establish-ments at Grande-Grave, one at Cap-des-Rosiers, two at Rivière-au-Renard and one at Cap-à-l'Ours, as well as a wharf, warehouses, store and hotel at Gaspé and several properties and mortgages in every Forillon settlement.17   He had also accumulated stocks and bonds in Montreal and Quebec banks and owned a house in Montreal where from 1874 he lived during the winter.   In 1875 he began turning over the administration of his establishments to his eldest son Isaac Elias, but kept financial operations in his own hands until his death.18   In 1919 Isaac's son Percival Gerald became managing director19 until the com-pany went bankrupt in 1967.20

The Company's Network of Fishing Stations

Hyman's correspondence shows how he ran his establishments, either personally or through agents and clerks. His correspondence of 1864 and 1865 indicates he was a very active man. He wrote more than 300 letters a year. He travelled regularly to his three main establish-ments at Grande-Grave, Rivière-au-Renard and Gaspé, and to Percé to settle legal matters.   Spring was a particularly busy time for him, getting everything ready for the fishing season: chartering ships, recruit-ing hired help, ordering merchandise, looking after advances to fisher-men, repairs, etc. (Appendix C).

By 1865 Hyman owned a large establishment at Grande-Grave, a wharf, general store and recently acquired warehouses at Gaspé, and five stations for unloading fish at Rivière-au-Renard, Cap-des-Rosiers, Anse à la Louise, Cloridorme and Mont-Louis (Appendix D describes these properties). It seems that only Grande-Grave and Rivière-au-Renard were both unloading and production centres for dried cod; the others were ports for unloading the catch and exchanging merchandise.21 Gaspé was also a centre for unloading winter fish, which was autumn fish either not dried or half dried and stored during the winter before the spring drying. It was also at Gaspé that salt imported from Spain and stocks of dried cod for export were stored. Most of the fish picked up by coastal schooners at different ports was sent to Gaspé. Ocean schooners hired by Hyman went directly to Grande-Grave and Rivière-au-Renard to load and unload, but they always had to go through customs at Gaspé before sailing for Europe.

Hyman exercised almost total control over his ports. Agents and clerks at the stations received all their instructions from him and had to go through him to get provisions. Clerks were salaried employees under Hyman and his agents. The agents at Rivière-au-Renard and Mont-Louis at that time were partners with him and received part of the profits as a commission or net profit at the end of the season (50%).22 Agents were buyers above all.   They had to set up a dealer system and were responsible for the agreements or contracts they made with their dealers. They were allowed a certain freedom in the price they paid for fish, depending on competition between local merchants. This was often quite brisk: Hyman wrote to his Mont-Louis agent who was having to put up with the Fruing company's "double dealings" at the time, "Get fish honestly if you can, but get fish, and as cheap as you can...."23

Hyman's agents and clerks were sometimes influenced by Fruing's, which made Hyman fear for his business interests. In 1865 in a letter to his Jersey broker he requested "Could you not send me a suitable young man by the Alice Jane this fall, as the one I now have goes home [Jersey] this fall, and besides he knows too much now, and visits too much my neighbours [Fruing]?"24

Fish were picked up at stations by coastal schooners owned independently or by Hyman. In 1865 he had at least two, the *Samuel* and the *Thistle*. They were used not only for picking up fish, but also for offshore fishing (at Anticosti especially) before going back to carrying fish in the fall.25 Merchandise from Quebec was shipped on schooners from Rivière-au-Renard (L.-A. Blouin), from Gaspé (Captains Ascah and Suddard) and Cap-St-Ignace (Captain Euloge Bernier).26 Captain Bernier was also in charge of bringing in workers "hired" for the season. The steamer *Lady Head* was also used: it made regular trips between Quebec and Gaspé.27

Shipwrecks, more frequent on the Gaspé north coast, were a significant source of income for Hyman -- at least profitable enough to offset losses in a bad fishing season. Ships that ran aground were sold at auction by Lloyds Insurance, and two or three merchants would often get together and share the cargo. In 1864 Hyman and the Blouin brothers from Rivière-au-Renard shared the profits from the sale of the cargo and rigging of two ships that ran aground at Cap-des-Rosiers.28

As an entrepreneur, Hyman was active in other areas as well. He had interests in the Banque nationale and the anque du Peuple in Quebec City, and in 1864 and 1865 he tried to have their banknotes circulated in the Gaspé and the north shore. But John Le Boutillier was strong competition; he had more influence with the banks than Hyman, who had to be satisfied with a more limited circulation.29

During his first thirty years of operation Hyman was in sole command of his enterprise. He was always on the spot and maintained longstanding personal relations with his dealers, which no doubt helped him to compete effectively with agents of the Fruing company.

Regional Importance of the Company

According to records of exports from the Port of Gaspé from 1852 to 1893 (Fig. 3), the volume of the Hyman company's exports grew between 1852 and 1864, as was the case for the total volume of exporters from the same port (Fig. 4). After that Hyman's volume of exports fluctuated considerably until 1875, reaching a new high in 1879 with 11 475 quintals of exported dried cod, after which they declined steeply. Between 1855 and 1890 the Hyman company accounted for an average of 9 percent of all exports from the Port of Gaspé, or about half of its main competitors, Fruing (20%) and the Collas brothers of

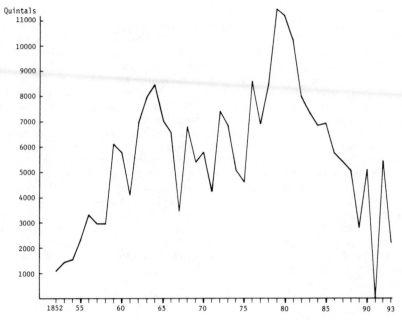

3. Cod exports of William Hyman and Sons, 1852-93.

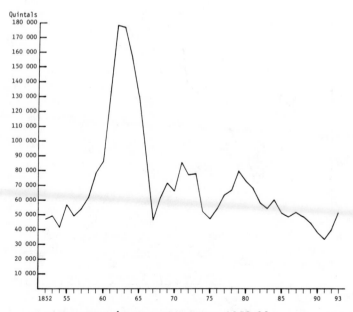

4. Gaspé port cod exports, 1852-93.

18

Pointe-St-Pierre (20%). Hyman was the fourth largest exporter after John Le Boutillier (15%). In 1855 these four companies accounted for 49 percent of all exports; by 1890 this figure increased to 94 percent (Table 1). These figures illustrate how production became concentrated in the second half of the century. It was only during the period 1861-66, when Gaspé was a free port30 and other merchants were able to enter the scene, that the relative share of the market by these companies decreased although the actual figures of their exports increased. But the extraordinary increase in exports during those years was mainly due to the fact that the Robin company of Paspébiac also took advantage of the free port and in 1861 registered there about 35 000 more quintals than the preceding year, and maintained that volume for the six years.

Hyman's importance as a merchant showed on the political scene. He was mayor of the township municipality of Cap-des-Rosiers from its founding in 1858 until its demise in 1882. He was also a county council member beginning in 1869, a captain of the militia and justice of the peace in the Gaspé district.31   In this capacity he had access to information at the Percé registry office, so that he knew all about his competitors' land transactions. In business competition, access to this information was extremely valuable.

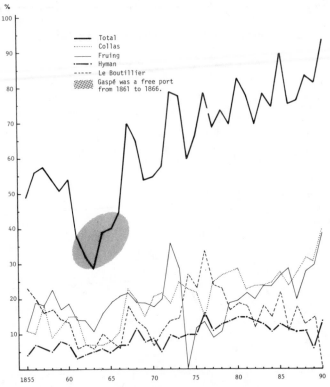

5. Relative importance of the four main Gaspé port exporters, 1855-90.

Table 1.   The relative share (%) of exports by the four main exporters from
the Port of Gaspé (1855-90).

Year	Fruing Co.	I. & E. Collas	J. LeBou-tillier	Hyman & Sons	Total
1855	11	11	23	4	49
1856	19	10	20	7	56
1857	18	18	16	6	58
1858	23	9	17	5	54
1859	17	12	14	8	51
1860	19	15	13	7	54
1861a	14	15	6	3	38
1862a	14	7	7	4	32
1863a	11	7	6	5	29
1864a	16	7	10	6	39
1865a	19	8	8	5	40
1866a	21	11	6	7	45
1867	22	23	18	7	70
1868	19	20	14	12	65
1869	19	15	12	8	54
1870	18	21	7	9	55
1871	20	22	11	5	58
1872	36	19	14	10	79
1873	29	25	15	9	78
1874	0	23	27	10	60
1875	12	22	23	10	67
1876	14	15	34	16	79
1877	9	25	24	11	69
1878	11	27	23	13	74
1879	19	20	17	14	70
1880	20	29	19	15	83
1881	22	23	18	15	78
1882	20	24	12	14	70
1883	24	24	18	13	79
1884	24	25	15	11	75
1885	27	28	22	13	90
1886	29	24	11	12	76
1887	20	28	18	11	77
1888	28	32	13	11	84
1889	30	31	15	6	82
1890	39	40	1	14	94
Avg.	19.80	19.86	15.19	9.33	64.19

a Gaspé was declared a free port from 1861 to 1866.

6. The Hyman and Fruing establishments at Grande-Grave in 1864. (David Hyman collection)

Position of the Company in the Commercial Structure

Because he spent so much time in the area, Hyman oversaw his growing number of dealers and establishments first hand, but his control over financing, provisions and exports was much weaker. Channel Islands' companies dominated these sectors, and we shall see how and under what conditions the Hyman company made inroads into their network.

Two important aspects must be remembered to understand the structure of the Gaspé fishing industry of the time. On the one hand, the great extent to which fishing could be exploited came from a massive influx of European capital in the Gaspé. Gaspé cod was an opportunity, especially for the Channel Islands' companies, to realize great profits on their capital. They invested in the production of dried cod and at the same time (which was just as important) in the yearly supply of Gaspé workers and fishermen. These European capitalists had thus succeeded in establishing a trading circle that profitably incorporated both the product and the necessary supplies for its production. On the other hand, the ports where production was concentrated were either directly controlled or financed by European capital. Hyman's case was the latter. The Robin and Fruing companies administered the Gaspé through their agents. Agents maintained contacts with local merchants, who acted as intermediaries between fishermen and the company. Hyman had direct links with his financing sources in Europe. Until 1862 his agent was the

Free & bonded warehouse and cold stores

Telegraphic Address : Salvamico - Naples
A. B. C. 5th & 6th Edit. Codes Used
Telephone 15 - 49

SALVIO & D'AMICO

IMPORTERS AND COMMISSION MERCHANTS

CODFISH - PILCHARDS - HERRINGS - PRESERVED FISH OF ALL KINDS
OILS AND ALL EDIBLE ARTICLES WOOL - CHEMICALS - DRUGS etc.

NAPLES, Italy
94, Via Marina Nuova
(Angolo Via Duomo)

NEW YORK.   ESTABLISHED 1902.   BOSTON.

SCARAMELLI & COMPANY

INCORPORATED

COMMISSION MERCHANTS

IMPORT AND EXPORT

32 North Moore Street,

NEW YORK

ESTABLISHED 1882.

STROHMEYER & ARPE COMPANY

IMPORT - & COMMISSION - MERCHANTS

SAPCO BUILDING.
139-141 FRANKLIN STREET,
NEW YORK.

7. Brokers of William Hyman and Sons at the beginning of the 20th century. (David Hyman collection)

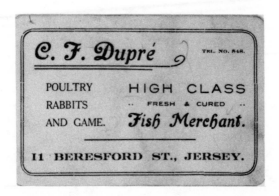

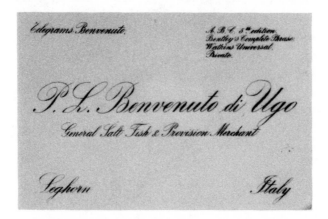

8. Importers and exporters of William Hyman and Sons' fish at the beginning of the 20th century. (David Hyman collection)

London brokerage firm of Janvrin, Grapée and DeLisle.[32] It went bankrupt that year and Hyman lost £2000. After that his agent was Samuel Dobrie and Sons in London and John Hardeley in Jersey.[33] Again from his correspondence we learn that in 1877 his agent was Ross Brothers in Liverpool;[34] he also did a lot of business with Montreal and Quebec banks at the time. In 1865 he paid 8 percent on advances he obtained from London and Jersey.[35] He did not get his provisions through Channel Islands' companies in Gaspé, but he had to go through brokers in Jersey to get to the market. Channel Islands' shipowners controlled all transportation and sales of cargoes. The main buyers of cod, especially in Italy, were also from the Channel Islands. The Jersey company Maingy and Robin controlled all cargoes going to the Mediterranean from their establishments at Civitavecchia and Naples.[36] The shipowners' control was all the more powerful in that it governed the beginning (financing) and end (outflow) of Hyman's production (Appendices E-G).

Hyman needed the alliance with the Channel Islands' companies, but he was vexed by his lack of control over his cargoes once they arrived overseas as well as the price of merchandise that was shipped to him. He was not the only Gaspé merchant caught in these constraints. Here is how he reacted to an increase in the price of gin in 1865: "My dear friend, there is a common saying on the coast, among the Jersey folks, that our Jersey dear friends want all."[37] In this quote he is referring to the clique of brokers and shipowners who controlled the distribution of goods and cod from Jersey.

One of Hyman's main interests was to get more control over the shipping of his cargoes. In the winter of 1864 he unsuccessfully tried to have them shipped from Halifax.[38] He also managed to ship them to other buyers in Italy, but this got him into trouble with the Channel Islanders: "That my fish has a bad name with M R & Co [Mainguy & Robin Company] at Naples I don't wonder at it, they are paying me off by ... ever since I once consigned to Pangratti."[39]

From the European capitalists' point of view, Hyman was a middleman who was both useful and bothersome -- bothersome because these capitalists wanted to control the entire cycle of cod production and sales; useful in that by financing him and selling his products, they were getting the best out of a situation in which part of the control was out of their hands. The Fruing company never failed to tell anyone who would listen to them that sooner or later they were going to drive him out, especially from the north shore: "... they say they will drive us out from up the River [St. Lawrence], let them try first, and my advice to them is, let them look out they may find breakers ahead."[40] Spreading these rumours was part of the game: Fruing company agents tried to scare fishermen who were doing business with competitors, sometimes even blackmailing the fishermen.[41]

European financial control became more apparent when Hyman had to face losses because of poor fishing seasons; he then could not pay his creditors. Two or three consecutive seasons could seriously endanger his business and inevitably he would have to bow to the good will of his creditors, as shown by this correspondence between John Hardeley and Samuel Dobrie and Sons of London, his two major creditors in 1868:

Mr. Hyman's position is much the same as for years past. He is struggling against bad sales. He has valuable property in Gaspé but not convertible in ready money convinced that our best & only good security was to keep him on his legs. ... This year he said you refused further advances & had I not assisted him he must have lost his season...[42]

Hyman desperately wanted to free himself from his dependence on outside financing and marketing of his production. In 1869 this desire seemed even more marked, to judge by the attitude of one of his creditors who wrote to him:

Believe me when I say that notwithstanding what may have passed & been done between us, which may have originated some crossed feelings -- My hope & desire is that you would grow independent of money lending which at best are a burthen and I think that by care and prudence you are in a position of freeing yourself in a few years.[43]

In the long run the company's survival was possibly linked to freeing itself from European capital. Shortly afterwards in fact, in 1873, a crisis developed in the capitalist world and several European companies went bankrupt, which led to the downfall of the Channel Islands companies in the Gaspé. Within the limits of this study we have not been able to assess the Hyman company's financial position at the time or how it survived the crisis. It did, however, outlive all the Channel Islands' companies in Gaspé Bay, and in 1918 and 1925 acquired the Fruing company's main establishments.[44]

William Hyman's personality, his tenacity and enterprising spirit wre significant factors in maintaining and developing his company, but these factors alone cannot explain all the social relations that existed between the merchant and the fishermen. His activities were part of a large commercial system, and the following chapters examine how this system adapted to the production of dried cod.

II PRODUCTION OF DRIED COD: TECHNICAL ASPECTS AND WORK FORCE

Factors Limiting Production

Merchants and planters who based their operations on the Gaspé fishery had to contend with several ecological, technical, economic, social and demographic factors that constantly hampered dried cod production. The very location of Gaspé places certain limits on resource extraction. At the time the merchants took over the fisheries, Gaspé did not have the infrastructure necessary to ensure production and supply. This deficiency, combined with the area's small population shortly after the British conquest, was critical in shaping the region's development in the 19th century. The main limitations on the various aspects of production were:

(1) the ecological (climatic) limitation, caused by the short Gaspé fishing season, which was never longer than five months (May to September) for the following reasons: access of small craft to fishing banks and of ships to coastal ports was blocked by ice; conditions were suitable for drying fish only during the summer; in the autumn, the cod leave the Gaspé Coast for the more southerly waters off Nova Scotia;

(2) lack of development in the methods used in coastal fishing was a factor in restricting the cod fishery to a strictly seasonal activity (technical limitation);

(3) because of prevailing technical conditions, the only way to increase production was to increase the number of workers; production was directly dependent on a resident population, augmented at times by seasonal workers;

(4) the qualifications and skills required of a labour force engaged almost exclusively in the production of dried cod influenced the ethnic origins of the Gaspé Bay population; the first planters to operate successfully in the area were Jersey and Guernsey Islanders;

(5) fishing gear and salt were essential to production; neither was available in Gaspé -- gear had to be imported from England and Scotland, salt from Spain;

(6) because the fishing season was short and the entire work force engaged in the production of dried cod, all supplies had to be brought in from England and Quebec City, making self-sufficiency impossible in several vital areas;

(7) dried cod was produced solely for export (mainly to Mediterranean countries); shipping the product to consumers required a broad-based transportation infrastructure, beyond the means of the individual producer;

(8) fish processing required suffcient beach space for the installation of stages, storehouses, dryers and flakes; control of the available space was a prerequisite to steady production.

These limitations constituted the major concerns of Gaspé merchants. They were facts of life that could not be ignored if the resource was to yield a profit. Depending on conditions (fishing season, economic situation), the organizational limitations directly affected the merchants' ability to obtain the capital they required for operating expenses. This was in itself a serious limitation, as the case of William Hyman demonstrates.

Due to these limitations, a vast commercial exploitation system was created in Gaspé centered on a single product (dried cod); it is this special type of production with its constraints that, no doubt, contributed most in the making of the Gaspé society in the 19th century.

Working Methods and Procedures

Types of Fishing

In the 19th century there had been little change in the method of fishing for cod or in fish processing procedures since the 16th century; descriptions dating from the 16th through 19th centuries of fishing and processing methods used to produce dried cod are virtually identical. Any changes over the centuries have been mainly in transportation and type of fishing. Boats and gear have undergone considerable change, but some men have always fished from large boats carrying fishermen, dressers and salters, and others from small one-, two- or three-man boats (called "chaloupes pêcheuses" by the French). As a result, there have always been both offshore ("migrante") and coastal ("sédentaire") fishing. The greatest differences between the two types are in the vessel, length of trip, number of fishermen carried and end product (salt cod or dried cod). The best example of offshore fishing is fishing off the Grand Banks of Newfoundland. Large vessels were outfitted and crewed (sailor-fishermen, dressers, salters) in European ports; fishing and processing were carried out on board. When the hold was full of cleaned and salted fish, the ship returned home. Later, vessels carried small two-man boats, or "dories," nested on their decks; the dorymen fished the banks all day, returning to the mother ship only at night.

In coastal ("sédentaire") fishing, temporary processing equipment was set up (stages, flakes, etc.) on the beach and the fish to be processed was landed in small two- or three-man boats. Unlike the large vessels that spent several days at sea (necessitating on-board salting to preserve the product), small boats made daily trips to the banks just off the coast. The French carried these boats in pieces, and had them assembled here by a carpenter. It was an era of strict division and specialization of labour. Dressing was the exclusive preserve of the ship's officers, and sailors were given the job of drying. Another class of workmen were the bait fishermen, whose sole job was to keep cod fishermen supplied with bait.[1] Coastal fishing was carried out solely for the production of dried cod; it became more and more widespread as the population along the shores of the St. Lawrence grew.

In the mid-19th century, coastal fishing in two-man boats was the norm in Gaspé. There was also some offshore fishing by men aboard schooners. This practice is mentioned in the correspondence and ledgers of the Hyman company.[2] The fishermen worked in "clubs," each one bearing the name of a schooner. The clubs were supplied by the company and they fished along the north shore and around Anticosti Island. This was not offshore fishing as we know it today, that is, on the high seas; it was simply coastal fishing involving trips of several days to a more distant coast. The cod was salted on board and sold by the draft[3] to the company. Schooner fishing was not widespread. The schooners also did some shipping along the Gaspé coast during the season. The longer trips were made early in season or when fishing was poor at Gaspé. To summarize, two types of fishing were carried out by the fishermen of Gaspé Bay, with coastal fishing in small boats by far the more common. Fishing on the banks and long fishing trips were made mainly to make up for seasonal lows of local fishing.

Resource Fluctuations

The Gaspé fisherman was vulnerable to fluctuations in the resource. The Gaspé coast cod fishery depended entirely on the cod's spawning migration to the northwestern Gulf of St. Lawrence between spring and fall. These migrations were not regular, and no scientific information on reproduction and migration of marine life was available then. If migrating cod were later than usual, or followed a different route, coastal fishermen had a poor season. Table 2 shows that even over a short period, ecological variation was important. The cod fishery was also completely dependent on the catch of bait, mostly capelin and herring.

Fishing depended, therefore, on the parallel, often unsynchronized, movements of several species; both route and time of arrival varied from season to season. William Hyman often mentioned in his correspondence that bait was plentiful but cod was scarce, especially at the beginning of the season; later in the season there would be no bait, but plenty of cod.[4] Unless a fisherman wanted herring for food, it seemed pointless to stock up on it for the coming season; it was said that cod disliked salt bait and took only fresh:

> for it must be borne in mind that there is no fishing without fresh bait -- the cod not being at all partial to salt fish. It is only on the great banks where the cod feeds chiefly on crustacea and mollusca that it bites at all freely at a line baited with salt herring or salt capelan.[5]

Whether this is an accurate description of variations in the cod's behaviour is difficult to prove; the fact that everyone believed it was probably sufficient to prevent anyone from stocking up on bait.

Fluctuations in the resource supply had serious social and economic repercussions. Planters and merchants had no accurate means of forecasting the coming season. All provisions for supplies, chartering

28

Table 2. Variations in the cod fishery (Rapports Fortin, (1854-63).[a]

Year	Variations	Locality
1854	--	--
1855	summer(+) fall(+)	Gaspé
1856	summer(+)	Cap-des-Rosiers
1857	summer(-) fall(-)	Gaspé
1858	fall(-)	Gaspé
1859	summer(+) fall (-)	from Rivière-au-Renard to Anse-au-Griffon(+) Douglastown(-)
1860	summer(+) fall(+)	Gaspé
1861	summer(-) fall(-)	Gaspé
1862	summer(+) fall (-)	from Rivière-au-Renard to Anse-au-Griffon(+) Pointe-St-Pierre and Mal-Bay(-)
1863	summer(-) fall (+)	from Rivière-au-Renard to Cap-des-Rosiers(-), from Chaleur Bay to Cap-des-Rosiers(+)

[a]Fortin's assessment was based on the quantity of cod and bait in stock during the season and on the average cod catch by boat. It is difficult to assess a fishing season accurately because we have no criteria by which to distinguish a good season from a poor one.
+Good season.
-Poor season.

ships, advancing money or goods to fishermen and hiring seasonal workers were made in winter and spring (Appendix C). If the cod were late or fewer in number, a planter's risks were higher, even more so if there were several poor seasons in succession. William Hyman illustrated the precariousness of the situation in a letter to a supplier:

> For goodness sake be pleased not to send me anymore goods at present. I am by far overstocked and nothing selling, at least nothing to get paid with. I fear the year of plenty is passed with us, and we are the years of scarcity.[6]

Local (intraregional) variations also had their effect on competition between firms; many failed in a relatively short time for just such reasons. On a larger scale, another gulf area (Newfoundland or Nova Scotia) would have an advantage in the marketplace if conditions were poor in Gaspé; the reverse was, of course, also true. Merchants were aware of this, as illustrated in this excerpt from a letter sent by William Hyman in 1865, a poor season: "It is certainly a dangerous business this season, as it appears there was good fisheries made on the Newfoundland coast and elsewhere".[7]

A poor season was also disastrous for the fishermen, although when fish were scarce they did obtain a higher price for the fish they managed to catch. In 1867 many fishermen were in dire straits and the government was obliged to take steps to provide them with food.[8] In this context, a fisherman's debt would rise and his possessions become liable to seizure by the merchants: "This is the third season the fishermen are doing very poorly about here, in consequence large amount of debts accumulating and remain on the books."[9] Further on he says: "Merchants have been doing for them last winter what them can't repeat this winter."[10]

Resources were the determining factor, because no one had the slightest control over them. A poor summer season (June 1 to August 15) could be offset by a good fall season (August 15 to October 15) by increasing fishing effort in the fall. However, the fall season was usually less productive because weather conditions made frequent fishing trips impossible. After September 15, the weather became unsuitable for drying fish; salted fish that could not be sold on the Quebec and Montreal markets was stored in brine over the winter and dried the following spring.

Fishing Grounds[11]

In its migration toward Gaspé and its search for herring and capelin, the cod rose from its demersal habitat to a more pelagic level. It could then be fished in shallower water, especially on the banks near the projection of Cape Gaspé. In the spring, the cod moved close to the landlocked shores of Gaspé Bay in their hunt for spawning herring and capelin. Thus the men fished in the bay in spring, on the banks in summer and in the bay again in the fall (when offshore fishing became more hazardous). As a general rule, there was no fishing more than two miles offshore because fishing farther from shore would involve more sailing than fishing. To sail was to be at the mercy of the weather. A gust of wind could easily swamp the small craft,[12] and a drop in the wind forced fishermen to row to shore.

Because they operated in sight of the coast, the fishermen navigated by taking bearings on two fixed points on shore a known distance apart. This allowed them to establish the exact location of their "marks" or fishing spots. Each bank had its marks, and all fishermen seem to have known where they were. Because fishing was by hand-line, no area was reserved for fishermen. Coastal fishing being what it was, the fishermen had no choice but to run along the coast when the fish were not biting in a particular area. The fishermen of Paspébiac and Bonaventure moved around considerably and usually ran up the coast to Percé near the end of the season.13 The cod traps used in Newfoundland and on the north shore of the St. Lawrence restricted the fishing ground, but these traps were never used in Gaspé.

The herring fishery did require allocation of the available space, and so location of herring nets was subject to regulation. The herring were caught in floating gillnets moored just off the fishermen's beaches; too many of them in close proximity often resulted in conflict. Captain Fortin, the first fishery officer in the gulf, sometimes had to settle disputes between fishermen.14

Boats

The fishing boat was a small sailboat that had an eighteen- to twenty-two-foot keel and a five- to seven-foot beam. It was built like a whaling ship, rigged like a schooner and carried three working sails (mainsail, foresail and jib).15 It was a two-man boat, had no bridge and could hold three to five drafts of cod. A well-maintained boat could last six to eight years; it was not expensive because local materials could be used in its construction.16 The cost of a boat seems to have increased very slowly; in 1865 a boat sold for £8, the same as in 1777. It was in 1777 that Nicholas Cox pointed out that Gaspé fishermen had an advantage over Newfoundlanders, who had to pay up to £60 for a boat17 and also fish much farther offshore.

The population was spreading along the coastline and, in addition, all beaches were privately owned. The large fleets of fishing boats once moored off each beach became a thing of the past. The need for landing stages was not felt until the 20th century, when introduction of the marine engine and development of highway transportation resulted in the building of small local harbours. Mooring offshore involves using rowboats to land both catch and crew. These "flats" were twelve-foot rowboats which plied back and forth between fishing boat and shore. Large fishing establishments, like those of the Hyman and Fruing companies, had series of moorings chained together and firmly anchored to the bay bottom.

At the end of the fishing season the cod dried on the fishermen's beaches was delivered to the company for weighing, grading and pricing. The fishermen's accounts show that the price of a quintal of cod was based on whether or not a fisherman made his own deliveries. The entry "with coasting" means that the fish was delivered, in which case the fisherman received an additional six shillings a quintal. If a fisherman did not deliver, the company picked up his dried cod production in the coasting barges also used to convey goods to and from schooners. The company picked up the dried fish from the more distant beaches and its other fishing establishments in the fifty-ton coastal schooners that fished along the north shore and around Anticosti Island. McDougall (1979)18 says that most vessels built in Gaspé Bay were in fact fifty-ton schooners and also that several old established 18th century families specialized in building schooners, in coastal trade and in whale hunting.

9. Fishing barge, Forillon, ca. 1930.

The men who sailed these schooners were largely whole or part owners of the vessels. Merchants like William Hyman, William Fruing and John Le Boutillier also owned coastal schooners which they crewed with local men.19

Entries in the fishermen's accounts show some of them credited with a fishing boat or flat. There is no way of knowing whether any of the fishermen were also skilled boat builders. According to the information gathered in 1976,20 some fishermen did have a name as boat builders, but at the turn of the century many fishermen still built their own boats. The crediting of a boat to a fisherman was erratic and does not seem to indicate the existence of a boat-building industry as such. It seems more logical to assume that inclusion of boat building in the trading arrangements was the exception. It is also difficult to determine whether or not the company was in the habit of ordering a boat from a fisherman who was heavily in its debt. Boats were undoubtedly built as required; it is entirely possible that when a company or one of its dealers had to replace a boat, a builder was chosen on the basis of the size of his "obligation" to the company. Sail making and repair appear less frequently in fishermen's accounts and seem to have been skilled trades. Some of Hyman's dealers bought their sails ready-made, others bought canvas or sailduck. Gear and rigging were also purchased at the company's store.

Fishing techniques

As mentioned earlier, bait fishing is a prerequisite for hand-line cod fishing. It is bait fishing that required the highest investments by the fishermen (herring nets, mackerel nets, capelin seines). This gear accounted for the most costly items debited to a dealer, and its purchase produced a sizeable increase in his account. Between 1854 and 1864, a herring net cost from £5 to £6, a mackerel net from £4 to £5 and a capelin seine from £12 to £20, the equivalent of twelve to twenty quintals of cod. The most common purchases were herring and mackerel nets. The companies had seines that were used to keep their hired fishermen supplied with bait; fishermen sometimes formed "clubs" for the purchase and use of a seine, which required at least seven men to handle.21 The fishermen were obliged to purchase nets for a variety of conditions; for example, nets of different sizes (from 2-in. to 2 1/4-in. mesh) were needed because of variations in herring size from one season

10. Taking herring out of the nets at Grande-Grave, ca. 1900.

to another. Hand-lines, hooks and leads were also purchased from the company, but their cost was negligible (seven to ten shillings for a pair of lines) compared with the cost of nets. About 1860, Hyman's dealers rarely trawled for cod.   In 1866 William Hyman equipped several schooners with specially ordered trawl nets.22   In 1868 the fishery officer spoke of discussions in Gaspé about prohibiting trawling, as the French had done in Newfoundland;23 However, in 1874 he noted that trawling had begun again between Grande-Grave and Port-Daniel.24 Trawling seems to have been done exclusively from schooners.

    To summarize, the fishing method was relatively simple. The herring or mackerel nets were attached in series to a beam called a "mooring" and let down at the end of a day's fishing so the fish would become entangled during the night. Around the middle of the night, the fishermen raised the nets, detached them and sailed for the banks, preparing their bait for the lines as they went. When they arrived at their fishing spot, they lowered the sails and dropped anchor. The fishermen, one fore and the other aft, each threw one or two hand-lines over the sides of the boat. When the cod were biting, the lines were hauled in quickly as hooked cod do not struggle. The work was very monotonous and if a fisherman was at all ambitious, he had to have a great deal of stamina. The work was more strenuous when the fishermen had to do a "dégrat" (move from one spot to another in search of cod); if the wind dropped and the men were forced to row, it was harder still. Normally the fishing began about 3:00 AM and ended about 4:00 PM. Then the processing started.25

Processing

    The processing operation has often been described in detail.26 The method of drying cod had not changed perceptibly since Europeans first began fishing off the North American coast.   Fortin fives a complete description of 19th century methods.27   In the next chapter we shall examine the human resources required for the operation.   For the moment we shall describe the product itself and the climatic conditions required to produce it.
    Fish is dried by reducing its moisture content to a minimum with three agents: salt, wind and sun. The only one of these subject to any degree of control is salt; wind and sun are factors of geographic location. In the last analysis, product quality, that is, degree of dryness, is determined by weather conditions. The Gaspé climate is ideal for the preparation of a quality product:

> It is on the coast of Gaspé where the effects of the mists generated by the Gulf Stream are least felt, that the finest Cod in all America is cured. It is well known on the markets of Spain and Italy, where it is preferred to all other fish.
> At Labrador, on the coasts of the Straits of Belle Isle, and at Newfoundland where for whole weeks, the fogs brought on by the easterly and north-easterly winds do not allow a single ray of the sun to be seen, Cod is cured with great difficulty, especially in the

11. Splitting cod on a family beach at Anse-aux-Sauvages, ca. 1930.

months of June and July; and the fish from those countries is always inferior to what which is despatched from the ports of Gaspé and New Carlisle.[28]

Fog is detrimental to the drying process because it increases the risk of bacterial growth. Bacteria are killed by adding salt, with the attendant risk of "burning" the fish. The Labrador and gulf stream currents meet around Newfoundland and produce heavy fog. This is why Newfoundland dried cod is an inferior product. There were serious problems involved in the establishment of a Gaspé fishery, as there were for any Gulf of St. Lawrence fishery; the favourable climate was a telling factor in the success of the Gaspé operations. If thousands of quintals of cod are to be set out in the wind and sun, large spaces must be available. This explains the eagerness of merchants, planters and companies to acquire the large beaches.

There are four operations involved in the production of dried cod: splitting, salting, washing and drying, each phase requiring specific materials and equipment. Splitting or dressing can be subdivided into three stages: throating, heading and actual splitting. Dressing was done at a table set up on the beach, or on the stage head in large fishing establishments. Next, the split cod was salted. In the large establishments, the cod was generally kench-cured. Independent fishermen usually soaked the cod in tubs of brine (pickle-cure).[29] Salt is the raw material that appears most frequently in fishermen's accounts. Gaspé fishermen preferred coarse salt to fine.[30] Transportation and storage oʻ salt was one of the major concerns of the large companies. At the beginning and end of the fishing season, salt was imported from Cadiz; the trip's profitability was ensured by carrying salt on the outgoing voyage and fish on returning to Spain. All the large companies operating in Gaspé Bay had huge storehouses in the port of Gaspé for salt, dried cod and other merchandise.[31] On the beaches salt was stored near the stage head where the salting was done. Washing, to remove any salt residue, was done by stirring the cod in huge troughs of fresh water. Drying was the most delicate of the operations. In the large fishing establishments, drying was supervised by a beach master who was in charge of all handling of cod by shoremen. Independent fishermen left the responsibility for drying to women, children and retired fishermen, while the head of the family went to sea. Several individuals who worked at a large beach (for example, Anse-St-Georges or Anse-aux-Sauvages at Forillon) would supervise the drying and their sons or partners fished and handled the processing.

After the fish had "taken its salt," it was dried by repeated exposure to the wind and sun. Between dryings, the cod were arranged in large piles or kenches to extract moisture by pressure. Drying and

12. Shore workers drying cod at Grande-Grave in the early 1900s.

kenching were repeated until the cod had reached the desired hardness. The fish were then sent to dry-stores and set out for one final drying before being loaded for shipment. Each time the fish was put out in the sun it was said to have had "a sun." Normally the entire process took from two to three weeks and, according to Fortin[32], Gaspé produced very little second quality cod, 5 or 6 percent; in a cloudy or rainy summer, the figure could reach 15 or 20 percent.

The entire procedure was based on simple work methods, simple operations and inexpensive equipment. The largest investments required were for boats and gear, nets, salt, stages and storehouses. Catch and processing methods were inefficient and the only way to increase production was to increase the labour force and make each worker a specialist. Sea work and land work provided a natural division of labour, although independent fishermen often did their own splitting and salting. In large establishments, there was always a clear-cut distinction between fishermen and shoremen. Subdivision of the work involved in actual fishing was possible only within large establishments; for example, cod fishermen could be supplied with bait by bait fishermen, or simply by shoremen who tended the nets.[33] Division and specialization seems more logical in processing; however, the strict timetable precluded overspecialization and the work force was always divided roughly into splitters, salters and shoremen. Because of the limits of the production method, increasing the labour force was the main factor in increasing production.

Work Force

Assessment of Work Force

Because the production process is enshrined by tradition, it lends itself to assessment of the labour force required for the fishing and processing operations. In speaking of the French offshore fishing operations in North America, Nicolas Denys (1672) and Duhamel Du Monceau (1769) estimate that five men were required per fishing boat, three of them fishermen, the other two shoremen.[34] These authors called the three fishermen "maître de bateau," "arrimeur" and "bossoint" (Denys); "maître de bateau," "avant de bateau" and "banquier" or "ussat" (mémoire de St. Malo -- 1786); that is, there was one man to steer, another to handle cargo and the third to handle ropes (mémoire Raudot et Duhamel du Monceau); "bossoint," "banquier" and "ussat" were names given to apprentice fishermen.[35] The number of boats was a factor of vessel tonnage. In 1686 at "l'île Percée" Intendant de Meulles set the ratio at one per twenty tons.[36] Du Monceau, writing in the 18th century, mentions the same standard.[37] Beach space was divided on the basis of the number of boats, allowing 2 1/2 "toises" (15 ft) of beach width for each boat and an area of "60-70 toises" in circumference for each boat, including beach space and space for flakes; the same rules applied to local fishermen.[38]

Two documents dating from the beginning of British rule mention standards for work crews and distribution of beach space used for splitting and drying cod. These are censuses taken by Lieutenant Governor Nicholas Cox -- the first in 1777, the second in 1784.[39] The first allows us to assess the size of the crews by listing the number of boats and the number of employees of each master fisherman. Table 3 gives the number of men per boat; the figures include persons listed as employees, male children over sixteen years old, and heads of families as master fishermen.[40]

Table 3.   Geographical distribution of boats and fishermen between Forillon and Bonaventure Island based on the 1777 census.

Locality	No. boats	No. men	No. men/boat
"Gaspée within the capes"	25	112	4.48
"Percée"	104	516	4.96
"Mal Bay"	8	35	4.37
"Island of Bonaventure"	9	44	4.88
Total	146	707	4.84

If we include the twenty-one women over sixteen years old, the average number of workers per boat would be 4.98, almost identical to the figure given by 17th and 18th century authors. We cannot know for certain that in Gaspé in 1777 every fishing boat carried three men. However, in the 19th century William Hyman's accounts (from 1854 on) and the fishery reports give the figure as two men per boat, a master fisherman and his helper. The third person could well have been a fisherman's young son, a practice still common at the beginning of the 20th century.[41]

The 1784 census for Percé and Bonaventure Island can be used to establish to thirty-six feet the fishing boat to beach space ratio. Of fifty-one users of the beach, thirty-seven had thirty-six feet of space, four had slightly more, the ten others slightly less. Divergence from the norm was probably due to removal and addition of boats after the original allotment of space. This would mean that beach space per boat was double that reported by Duhamel Du Monceau in 1769 (2 1/2 "toises," or 15 ft). It seems that under the French régime greater crowding of the beaches was permitted, probably because of the greater fishing effort by captains engaged in coastal fishing. Allocation of beach space seems to have been most common in Percé, where the Robin company owned nearly one-quarter of the beaches in the mid-19th century:

They [the Robins] have beautiful establishments; there are thirty buildings on their beach at Percé. They occupy nearly one quarter of the coves and have about 60 fishing boats, manned by men from Paspébiac.[42] (translation)

The allocation of space was typical of the seasonal fishing of the European and American vessels in the 18th century. In the 19th century, in a context of private property of the beaches, the number of fishing boats used depended on the storehouse capacity for fish waiting to be dried. An announcement of the sale of the Mahier company in Grande-Grave in 1820 says that the establishment included flakes with space to dry the catch of six boats.[43] About the mid-19th century, the five-man per boat standard appears in descriptions of work units. Each unit included two fishermen and three processors (throater, header and splitter).[44] As seen in the 1777 census, the average crew was made up of five men and most of the labour was done by seasonal workers. The norm of five men to a boat is thus based on a strict division of labour into fishermen and shoremen.

In 1777 the 5 to 1 ratio is also observed with the master fishermen who owned only one boat. Division of labour on that small a scale presupposes specialization. The standards seem to be based on long tradition, and change in the distribution of duties once a season had begun was rare. Lepage[45] cites a case reported in the minutes of the provincial court at Douglastown in 1809. A master fisherman wanted to transfer a man from fishing to splitting in mid-season. The man refused and the master, obliged to do the work himself, lost a construction contract as a result. The master won the case in the end and the employee had to pay him ₤20 for his losses incurred, the value of the contract. This harsh verdict is an example of the firm will of the dealers for departing from the restrictive traditional work norms peculiar to the development of fisheries in Gaspé.

In the first years his company was in operation, Charles Robin instructed a captain who was to hire fishermen in Jersey to be sure to hire "gens d'entreprise"[46] rather than "gens de règle." This again could be a clear indication of the problems facing merchant adventurers in the hiring of labour. If this is the case, it would appear that European fishermen also had rules concerning the duties of individuals in the production process. The merchants' habit of having the crews of transport ships fish for cod was the cause of bitter protests among sailors, and the practice had to be dropped.[47] This seems to indicate that the men who arrived in Gaspé to fish were not entirely at the mercy of the merchants, at least as long as they did not settle there. In the days when ships were outfitted in Europe to fish in Gaspé with a crew of seasonal workers, all duties had to be specified and assigned before departure. Even in a poor season, the outfitter had to fulfill his obilgations and pay his crew. When a master was dealing with permanent residents, there was no question of leaving his employees idle when they could not put out to sea. If the season was poor, the beach masters gave workers other work, in the fields, for example. All farm work was done and community services provided when fishing was poor. The case cited by Lepage is extreme, but it demonstrates that no opportunity for obtaining paid work could be lost and, more importantly, that the "rule" of days gone by was about to change.

At the beginning of the 20th century, the Fruing company of Grande-Grave still operated with a strict division between fishermen and shoremen.[48] Apparently several factors -- shortage of seasonal workers from outside the area, and an increase in local population -- blurred the previous rigid lines between the two categories of workers. Fishermen affiliated with a company beach were doing their own splitting at the end of the day; drying was still done by company shoremen. Also, both the organization and division of labour apparently underwent changes in the 19th century. Information available for the mid-19th century suggests that the norm of five men per boat dropped to three. From 1863 until 1885 inclusively, shoremen were included in fishery statistics, apparently to emphasize the importance of seasonal migration. But the number of shoremen given for each locality would not include members of independent family units, in particular women and children. Considering only shoremen included in the statistics, the number varied from 1 to 1.5 per fishing boat. Including the crew, that means an average of slightly over three men to a boat. The 1777 ratio of 5 to 1 was based on all residents old enough to work, including women and children; the 3 to 1 ratio is based on the number of workers counted by the fishery officer. Logically, on the independent beaches the ratio would be much higher if women and children were included. Although this is a possibility, the company fishing establishments at Grande-Grave should show a larger ratio because no women or children were hired for the season. And yet Tables 4 and 5 do not show any appreciable difference in ratio. The mid-19th century drop in the ratio from 5 to 1 to 3 to 1 can be attributed most probably to changes in the division of labour; the creation of huge company fishing establishments could have been aimed at greater rationalization of labour for increased productivity. Lack of data makes it difficult to judge the effect of labour reorganization within a specific industry; we do know that where manufacturers have brought skilled craftsmen in related fields together under one roof, rational division of labour has proven effective.

No data are available on the number of hours worked in the fishing industry, more particularly in fish processing. How many hours a day did shoremen work? Was splitting full-time work, or did splitters dry fish as well? Such information is needed for each time period under study if we are to assess the effect of possible changes in division of labour, including any increase in the length of the working day. Splitting and salting are jobs that lend themselves to specialization and increased effort. Some splitters were undoubtedly faster workers than others and performance would improve if a splitter did nothing but actual splitting (cleaned and headed cod and removed the backbone). In 1866 William Hyman sent a letter to his hiring agent at Cap-Saint-Ignace in which he specified one splitter, five shoremen, one cook and one salter for every five or six fishing boats.[49] If these figures represent the number of workers required to handle the production of five fishing boats, there were 1.4 shoremen per boat, 1.16 per boat if there were six boats. This corresponds to the Table 4 figures for Gaspé County.

Table 4 data plotted in Figure 13 show that the number of fishermen was directly proportional to the number of boats, not surprising if there were always two fishermen per boat. The number of shoremen per boat does not follow the same rule. From 1863 to 1880 (Fig. 13), the average number of shoremen per boat was one (0.96). The curve shows that as fishing effort increased (that is, the greater the

Table 4. Annual figures of number of boats, fishermen, shoremen, Gaspé County (1863-82).

Year	No. fishing boats	No. fishermen	No. shoremen	Avg. no. fishermen per boat	Avg. no. shoremen per boat	Quintals cod per boat
1863[a]	1383	2760	1309	1.99	0.94	85.19
1864[a]	1580	3146	1822	1.99	1.15	58.54
1865[a]	1923	3846	2491	2.00	1.29	63.68
1866[a]	2115	4230	2455	2.00	1.16	45.20
1867[a]	1909	3830	2278	2.00	1.19	57.33
1868[a]	1909	3830	2278	2.00	1.19	57.33
1869	1496	3362	1471	2.24	0.98	54.04
1870	1143	2351	1084	2.05	0.94	62.65
1871	1347	2584	1163	1.91	0.86	68.35
1872	1239	2344	1159	1.89	0.93	90.03
1873	969	2117	372	2.18	0.38	85.86
1874	1477	2301	639	1.55	0.43	50.27
1875	1292	2606	1078	2.01	0.83	64.54
1876	1501	3001	1391	1.99	0.92	58.44
1877	1668	3306	1674	1.98	1.00	60.41
1878	1670	3372	1694	2.01	1.01	56.82
1879	2055	4095	1976	1.99	0.96	64.66
1880	1624	3281	1550	2.02	0.95	60.98
1881	1181	2328	1004	1.97	0.85	
1882	1316	2394	726	1.81	0.55	66.54

[a]The Magdalen Islands are included from 1863 to 1868.

numbers of fishermen and boats), the number of shoremen per boat climbed above the average, and vice versa. For the last five years, the number of shoremen per boat remained near average despite a fishing effort equal to that of the first five years.

Because of the presence of seasonal workers, fishing effort could be adapted according to changes in the catch; furthermore, there was a specific minimum number of boats above which any increase or decrease in shoremen per boat affected the intensity and division of onshore labour. During this period the structure of the fishing industry depended greatly on the availability of seasonal labour. As long as the natural increase in local population could not keep up with the increased fishing effort introduced by the companies, local labour had to be augmented by migrant seasonal labour. In other words, the merchants, with the available capital, could hire more fishermen than the Gaspé population could supply and therefore hired migrant workers. Thus the amount of available capital determined the degree of the fishing effort, that is, the capacity to acquire more equipment and increase the labour force. The increased fishing effort meant increasing the credit to planters to hire more fishermen and seasonal workers and acquire more equipment. In

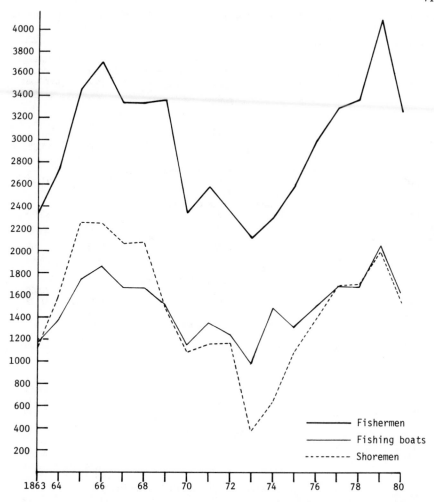

13. Fishing effort in Gaspé County, 1863-80.

such a context, not only the plants flourished but some small family plants could use a few additional fishermen for a season or two. If credit and fishing effort fell, planters who had piled up debts when times were good had to bear the brunt of these same debts when fishing effort was down. The capital used by the merchant in the credit system was, of course, a risk, but most of the risk was borne by the fishermen who, sooner or later, had to pay their debts to their creditor. An examination of the distribution of the labour force among the William Hyman company's dealers follows.

Table 5. Annual figures of number of boats, fishermen, shoremen -- Forillon Peninsula (1863-65).

Year	No. fishing boats	No. fishermen	No. shoremen	Avg. no. fishermen per boat	Avg. no. shoremen per boat	Quintals cod per boat
			Grande-Grave			
1863	25	50	35	2	1.40	98.00
1864	38	76	55	2	1.45	70.00
1865	51	102	90	2	1.76	45.88
		Anse-St-Georges, Anse-aux-Sauvages, Longue Pointe				
1863	26	52	24	2	0.92	91.53
			Longue Pointe to Shiphead			
1863	8	16	6	2	0.75	85.00
			Middle Cove and Anse-St-Georges			
1864	14	28	20	2	1.42	70.00
1865	43	86	53	2	1.23	52.79
			Anse-aux-Sauvages and Shiphead			
1864	34	68	40	2	1.17	70.00
1865	41	82	50	2	1.21	58.29
			Cap-des-Rosiers			
1863	40	80	25	2	0.62	60.00
1864	34	68	36	2	1.05	60.00
1865	40	80	50	2	1.25	35.00
			Anse à la Louise			
1863	13	26	9	2	0.69	49.61
1864	15	30	18	2	1.20	60.00
1865	20	40	25	2	1.25	55.00
			Anse-au-Griffon			
1863	81	162	75	2	0.92	80.00
1864	37	74	45	2	1.21	65.00
1865	52	104	70	2	1.34	53.46
		Rivière-au-Renard and Petite Rivière-au-Renard				
1863	81	162	75	2	0.92	78.14
1864	82	164	99	2	1.20	58.41
1865	117	234	147	2	1.25	52.00
Total						
1863	274	548	249	2	0.90	77.97
1864	254	508	313	2	1.23	63.60
1865	364	728	485	2	1.33	50.45

Local Fishermen and Migrant Workers

The work involved in the production of dried cod -- on shore and at sea -- depended on both local population and migrant workers. In general, residents owned or had access to a beach and had their own

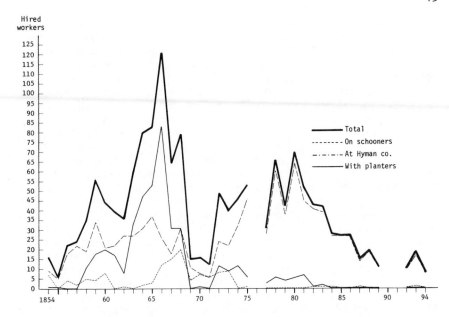

Hired
workers

125
120
115
110
105
100
95
90
85
80
75
70
65
60
55
50
45
40
35
30
25
20
15
10
5
0

1854   60   65   70   75   80   85   90   94

——— Total
------- On schooners
—·—·—· At Hyman co.
——— With planters

14. Employees of William Hyman and Sons, 1854-94.

boats, fishing gear and processing equipment. The migrant population
was made up of seasonal workers who formed the labour force of the
company fishing establishments and sometimes joined members of local
family units in fishing and processing cod. The fisheries had been
organized along these lines since the beginning of British rule in Gaspé,
and it was not until the last quarter of the 19th century that migrant
workers began to disappear from the area. Around 1860, migrant
workers still played an important role in production and their numbers
directly affected production. The number of permanent residents was
increasing steadily, but available capital could finance a higher level of
production than local residents could handle. Most of the seasonal
workers were wage earners and their cost for the season could be
forecast; residents needed annual advances of goods, even when fishing
was poor. A seasonal labour force was a short-term, controlled
investment for a company; investment in the form of advances to a local
labour force was long term, and involved risks that were often unpre-
dictable. Residents cost a company more, yet they were the cornerstone
of the production process; this is why the companies kept them on such a
tight rein.

Residents

The place of residents in the structure of the fishing industry is
discussed in several mid-19th century documents. Historians have
always based their descriptions of the fisherman's social condition on

impressions gathered by travellers, and so we have the stereotype of the poor fisherman enslaved by his debts to the merchant. Historians have not gone beyond the duality of the misery of fishermen and the totality of merchant control. A more in-depth study shows the social distinctions between fishermen. There were, however, varying degrees of dependence on the merchants; a fisherman's place in the structure determined his ability to weather a poor fishing season and its repercussions on the merchant system. A fisherman's social position depended first and foremost on the location of his property. If he had access to a sheltered beach fairly near the fishing grounds, this gave him a credit advantage in addition to the physical one. Access to a good fishing spot depended on several factors: the age of the fishing establishment, obtaining a piece of land, the availability of capital, the fisherman's skill, the composition of his family and his solvency. A fisherman who had no access to a beach had two choices: to get hired by someone else (planter) or go into partnership with other fishermen. From the point of view of a merchant providing advances, a planter was a better risk than an individual fisherman. If a planter did go too far into debt, he owned property that could be seized; the company could force him to sell his "room," and resell it to a dealer it considered a better risk. A company or merchant had nothing to gain by evicting a fisherman who had no property. Merchants tended to deal with planters, making them responsible for hiring and giving advances to individual fishermen, who were then the planter's responsibility. The responsibility for company advances was thus divided; if a planter was in financial difficulty with a merchant, he was held responsible for "his" fishermen's debts. This is the standard model for distribution of advances in Gaspé, especially in the Chaleur Bay area. The model was not a hard and fast rule; the Hyman company's dealings with its customers illustrates some of the exceptions. As long as company fishing establishments and planters could absorb the entire local labour force, the fishing industry continued to be organized according to this model. But when merchants were competing for planters and the population was growing and expanding, merchants were obliged to deal increasingly with fishermen who did not always meet their financial criteria for planters. This seems to have been the case with William Hyman, whose customers were largely small independent producers.

Pierre Fortin, fishery officer from 1852 to 1867,[50] was in an excellent position to observe the organization of labour. His descriptions correspond closely with a model of the organization at a large fishing establishment. He describes a typical establishment but makes no mention of social distinctions. He makes no reference to a structure in which planters were middlemen, nor does he go into detail concerning the company system of distributing advances. In 1856, speaking of the Grande-Grave fishing establishments, he wrote that half the companies' production came from company plants and was produced by seasonal labour, the other half from fishermen who lived on the coast and were given advances against future production.[51] On numerous occasions Fortin was called on to settle cases involving "desertion" by a fisherman who had received an advance from his master or shipper. By "master," Fortin seems to have meant any person who provided advances, that is, a merchant or a planter. The following interesting example of such a case illustrates the severity of the penalty for desertion:

> On the 14th, I sat in court in Percy, with Dr. Konick, a Justice of the Peace of the District, to try five fishermen who were charged with having broken their engagement. Their guilt having been fully proved, they were sentenced to pay a fine of ten dollars each, or to be imprisoned for twenty days, and as they did not pay the fine, they were all sent to Percy Gaol.

Fortin adds:

> I must here remark that such an example as this could not fail to produce a salutary effect among the people of the coast by showing that if any of them should be inclined to break their engagment, after having received from their shippers considerable advances in fishing tackle, and especially in provisions, justice would overtake them and punish them for their bad faith; but would also protect them against any unworthy treatment from their employers, if need were.[52]

These fishermen were not being used to set an example, for Fortin had earlier handed down the same decision.[53]   Fortin's authoritarian decisions demonstrate the courts' support and guarantee of the merchant system.

In 1857 the missionary assigned to Percé, L'Abbé Gingras, gave a more detailed description of the organization of the fishing industry and its inherent social distinctions. He said in part:

> The fishery occupies all the men, women and young women and all children able to do a little work. Like any industry, fishing has its rich and its poor. Those who built in the coves, who have a place to anchor their boats, are well off. The others are nothing but miserable wretches unable to wrest a living from the sea. Those who have fishing stations generally own 2, 3, 4 or 5 boats and are called planters. They provide the fishermen with solid, well-built, nicely painted, well rigged boats that are very light and skim over the water, for the fisherman loves his boat above all else, and must have it clean and shipshape. The planter hires men to crew his boats; the boats carry two men called half-liners; each of them keeps one quarter of the catch, the other half going to the planter. The fishermen provide their lines and food. The planter gets half the catch and all the oil, pays the expenses and is responsible for processing. The fisherman throws the cod on the shore, and later finds it processed in the store. A planter's expenses are high and only those who are good managers and are lucky enough to hire good fishermen make any profit. It costs £20 to equip a boat. A planter also needs 8 to 10 herring nets, at $12 to $15 each, for it is his responsibility to provide his fishermen with bait.... He also needs seines, which are very expensive, and extensive buildings for making fish [processing].

In addition, he runs great risks; he must hire his fishermen in March. These men are extremely poor and hire themselves out in order to provide for their families. The planter gives each one an advance of about ten louis. Once the fishing begins, he must feed the fisherman and his family, who take advantage of the opportunity to eat heartily. If fishing is poor, a fisherman often remains in the planter's debt for a considerable sum that the planter will

15. Monsieur Bichard, a Forillon fisherman of Guernsey descent, 1922. (National Museums of Canada)

never see. A planter often loses boats and nets in bad weather and must allow for losses; at the present time, no-one can live with dignity by fishing alone. To live well, a planter must also farm the land. His servants [shoremen, who usually process fish] work the land on days when there is little processing to be done. The abundant supplies of seaweed and fish offal are used as fertilizer. The grain harvested is magnificent and is used to feed the animals, which in turn provide more fertilizer; the earth provides them with a multitude of goods which they were previously obliged to buy from the merchants, the scourge of these poor people.

The Jersey merchants run all the businesses and have an almost total monopoly. It is they who set the price of fish. "This year" says a merchant, "we will give you so much per quintal of cod" and there is no use complaining. The Robin Company fixed the prices for the whole coast and the "habitants" have no choice but to

16. Marc Packwood and Rachel O'Connor, of Irish descent, Cap-des-Rosiers, 1908. (Léo Packwood collection, Cap-des-Rosiers)

accept it -- every last one of them is in the merchants' debt...54
(translation)

L'Abbé Gingras describes the situation clearly; he distinguishes fisherman, planter and merchant, and points out the extent of the planter's
responsibilities. He also mentions employees who process fish. Thomas
Pye, in the text accompanying his engravings of Gaspé, speaks of the
production of the Robin company's beach masters and describes three
methods used to pay Paspébiac fishermen (draft, half-line and wages).
Everywhere he went, Pye described only large company fishing establish-
ments.55

Examination of the records, in particular the ledgers, of the Hyman
company verifies information provided by observers of the period and
describes in greater detail the organizational structure of the fishing
industry.

Planters
The first indication of a resident company dealer is the length of time
his account is open (January to December), the second that his balance is
carried over from one year to the next. Migrant workers' accounts were
opened at the end of May or the beginning of June and closed in
September or October.

There are two ways of recognizing a planter in a ledger: the size of
his yearly account (£100 or more) and the existence of accounts for
employees hired on his behalf by the company. An employee was
identified by having his master's name listed after his own, for example,
"Euloge Bernier at Geo. Innes." Certain details in a producer's debit and
credit columns are further indications of a planter:

> **debits**
> payment of expenses for hiring workers
> payment of wages ("paid your men", etc.)
> payment of travel expenses and supplies for employees
> large sums for advances
> large purchases of salt and fishing gear
> large cash deposits
> numerous advances on behalf of other persons
>
> **credits**
> large numbers of quintals of cod (over 100)
> number of quintals listed by boat (Euloge's boat, Gilbert's boat)
> discount on advances

These entries suggest a person who supervised a sizeable labour force,
had high expenses and a high level of production.

Fishermen
The individual fisherman is recognizable first by the absence of planter
attributes. His debit includes only "normal" advances for gear, salt,
food, clothing, etc., and his credit is based solely on his personal cod
production. His account is open year-round and the balance, usually

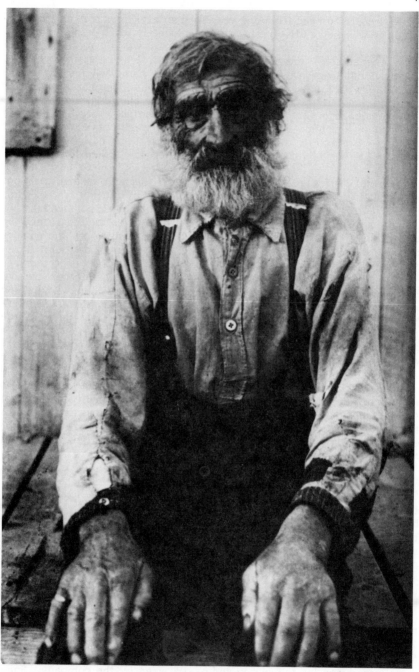

17. Monsieur André Fortin (77 years old), a French-Canadian fisherman from Cap-aux-Os, 1936. (National Museums of Canada)

negative, carried over from one year to the next. It is often difficult to establish whether a fisherman worked alone, in partnership or as an employee. In some cases, clearly a fisherman worked for a particular planter because his (the fisherman's) name will be given as the person to whom an employee was assigned. After his name will be listed, for example, "with Euloge Bernier." A link between fisherman and planter can sometimes be traced through an entry in the planter's account which, for example, refers to "Gilbert's boat," while another entry lists supplies provided to a certain Gilbert whom we think might have worked for a planter. A planter's debit column often refers to cash advances to individuals; the individual's account may be cross-checked for confirmation.

Some entries give the names of two fishermen as affiliated not with a planter but with one another, as indicated by the word "with"; this type of entry points to a simple partnership, but not all partnerships are indicated in this way. Their existence can often be confirmed by comparing shipments of fish from several fishermen; where the number of quintals delivered by two, three or four fishermen is identical, it can be assumed that these men caught and processed their fish as partners.

Many fishermen have no obvious link with any other person. Possibly these men worked either with a son or a man who had no account with Hyman, in which case he would not appear in Hyman's ledgers. Most local fishermen delivered a finished product to the company, that is, dried cod by the quintal. Others made daily draft deliveries of fresh or salted cod; during the time under study, the latter were the exception. The practice was more common at the beginning and end of the season, but never involved large amounts. Several residents worked for wages, generally in the fall, but again these were in the minority. The major portion of a fisherman's credit consisted of several quintals at the end of the summer season and less at the end of the fall season. The occasional resident was paid a wage during the entire fishing season; some were hired in winter for maintenance work at a farm or fishing establishment.

Mariners

Captains may sometimes be recognized by examining accounts opened in the name of schooners; the name of the captain is sometimes given beside the name of the schooner. If not, his name will be mentioned in transfers to his personal account from that of the schooner. A sailor is identifiable either from an item in a schooner's account that reports payment to him of a wage or share, or from a transfer from a schooner's account into his personal account. As stated earlier, schooners were used for both fishing and transport; in the ledgers, a schooner's credit balance may include items for fish produced by the crew as well as payments for delivery only. A schooner's crew often formed a "club" before leaving on a fishing trip. In such cases the club has an account and the crew's production is credited either to the club or the schooner. Most of the sailors were residents, often sons or brothers of the captain; some were hired for the season and paid a wage by the company. Some of these sailors were local residents, others were outsiders. William Hyman, in a letter offering to outfit a captain's boat for a fishing trip to

Anticosti Island, mentioned adding two "fishing crews" to the regular crew.[56] These fishing crews were made up of sailor-fishermen whom Hyman hired as other servants. Schooner fishing was far less common than fishing from two-man boats. Fisheries statistics list schooners and sailors from 1866 to 1885; this type of fishing declined sharply after 1890.[57] The fishery officer, in his annual survey of Gaspé Bay, reports that schooner fishing was most common among Douglastown fishermen who had little available beach space and were a relatively long way from the fishing grounds.[58]

Skilled Workers

The large company fishing establishments required the services of various skilled workers, especially for the construction and maintenance of fishing boats and for barrel making. Several coopers delivered barrels to William Hyman, and in every ledger there is an account for a carpenter, a blacksmith and a cobbler. There is sometimes mention of fishermen entrusted with making and repairing sails and nets; they are not referred to as skilled labourers as they did this work only in winter and spring. Some skilled workers also produced dried cod. We do not know whether they took part in the production directly, or owned boats from which their sons or employees fished.

Women and Children

Writers of the period tell us that women worked at splitting and more especially at drying cod on family beaches. Their work is not directly accounted for, but rather included in the production of head of the family. On rare occasions a fisherman's account includes remuneration for work done by his wife; the type of work is never specified. There are

18. Women drying cod on a Gulf of St. Lawrence beach at the beginning of the 20th century. (Marie Décarie collection)

several items for remuneration to a farmer's wife hired for the winter, undoubtedly for housework in William Hyman's home. When the Hyman family began moving to Montreal for the winter, they always took a Grande-Grave girl with them. Among the records of William Hyman is a small account book dated 1882 which includes company accounts for several women who were hired to cook for the fishermen and shoremen employed at the company's fishing establishment.

In 1976 an ethnographic survey was conducted at Forillon concerning the cod fishery at the turn of the century. Several fishermen mentioned a woman, a Newfoundlander, who could split cod as quickly and efficiently as any man. Several old iconographic dcouments show the work done by women at the splitting table. In the twentieth century, large fishing establishments (of both companies and planters) disappeared, resulting in subdivision and decentralization; this probably explains why women began to perform more specific fish processing tasks. In the mid-nineteenth century their work seems to have been limited to drying per se, the organization of fishing and processing being based largely on the large seasonal labour force. L'Abbé Gingras seems to contradict himself on the subject of work and women. At one point he says that "the fishery occupies all the men, women and young women, and all children able to do a little work." Further on he says that

"The women are lazy, do no housework, and are spendthrifts. They spend their days strolling up and down the roads, showing off and depriving themselves of nothing during the fishing season, even though they suffer later. Their greatest pleasure is drinking tea, and the only thing that bothers them is to be without it."[59] (translation)

When we study a population from an economic standpoint, the tendency is to presume that the people were by nature hard-working; it is difficult to see them as other than worthy, industrious folk cruelly exploited by greedy merchants. The generalized intensification of labour, especially during the industrial revolution, has shown that the picture is accurate, at least in the case of urban workers engaged in production within a capitalist system. The intensification of labour in the 19th century could not be as systematic in a seafaring context as in the cities, first because of climatic limitations, but also because of a certain flexibility in the various aspects of production; the important difference here is that production was largely the direct responsibility of producers. The work done by the fishermen was not directly subject to capital; they were not wage earners. This does not of course preclude exploitation of fishermen by merchants in the long term.

To return to the women, their work was confined mostly to processing; there were probably wide variations from one woman to another, according to family size, place on the social scale (wife of planter, wife of fisherman) and skill. Judging by the number of yards of material debited to fishermen's accounts, the women must have spent much of their time dressmaking. Some women apparently did this type of work exclusively; there are records of numerous payments to women for dressmaking. The children also helped in the drying process. A fisherman's account often includes payment for work done by his son, especially in the fall when huge quantities of cod filled the large fishing establishments and the final drying had to be finished before shipment. The children and other part-time employees were paid by the day or half-day, the item being recorded as "work at fish." Boys probably began their apprenticeship with their fathers at an early age, although the 1861 census does not list any male child under sixteen years old as a fisherman. In that year William Hyman's youngest fisherman-dealer was nineteen; the usual minimum was twenty-one, the age of maturity.

Migrants

Nearly all mid-19th-century migrant workers were French-Canadians from Montmagny, Cap-St-Ignace, L'Islet and Kamouraska. These people are the forbears of the French-Canadian population of Gaspé. Most of the "Canadiens" settled on the north shore of the Gaspé Peninsula where there was space available; the fishing stations on Chaleur Bay and Gaspé Bay continued to hire large numbers of "Canadiens" every year until sometime in the 1870s. Around 1880 the "Canadiens" from these areas were not the fishing establishments' only source of seasonal workers. Increases in local population and economic dependence on the companies combined to create a salaried labour force among Gaspé residents. It seems that the merchants preferred to hire seasonal workers -- perhaps their productivity was greater. In the last quarter of the 19th century great changes took place in the Quebec labour market; competition among various industries was high, and thus the "Canadiens" could demand higher wages. In 1883 Isaac Hyman, who had replaced his father William as manager of the firm, wrote to a hiring agent that the "Canadiens" he had requested were demanding higher wages than he was prepared to pay and he had decided to hire local fishermen.[60] In the mid-19th century (between 1850 and 1870) there were no serious hiring problems and the number of men hired depended on William Hyman's requirements and available funds.

The hiring of fishermen and shoremen was done by an agent from Cap-St-Ignace or L'Islet. Generally, Hyman dealt only with agents familiar with his requirements, although he sometimes dealt directly with fishermen who applied to him. In about 1860 Captain Euloge Bernier of Cap-St-Ignace was a personal friend and confidant of William Hyman. It was not uncommon for Hyman to communicate with an agent through Captain Bernier, especially if he was in doubt about the agent's ability to hire the required number of men. In this way Hyman gave himself the option of having Captain Bernier choose another agent if the usual one did not produce results. Earlier correspondence shows that Hyman and his son occasionally met with the agent during winter trips to Quebec City.[61]

There is not always a clear enough indication of an agent's social position in his own village to enable us to assess his ability to mobilize a labour force; we do know that, in Gaspé, the agent was usually a splitter, and thus a respected man.[62] In the company books, an agent can be recognized by credit given for hiring men. There are entries such as

"Hiring 12 men for W.H."; "Hiring of 19 men at 5/." An agent received five shillings for each man he hired and was also reimbursed for the men's travel expenses from Quebec City to Gaspé. The expenses included steamer passage and provisions, for example: "Provisions to 9 shoremen at 9/; 5 fishermen at 10/"; and "paid expenses from St-Ignace to steamer 5/each 20 men." Travel expenses were sometimes paid by Hyman's Quebec City agent, Thomas Fraser, even by the men themselves, in which case they were given credit with Hyman. There are entries for "passage down" or "provisions down," the word "down" meaning downriver to Gaspé. Agents were also given sums of money for advances to employees before their departure for Gaspé. Hyman sent advances directly to fishermen he knew personally; the agreement in such cases was usually reached the previous fall. Covering letters were all Hyman ever wrote in French.[63]

A letter to C. Ouellette was delivered by Captain Euloge Bernier, as were most of Hyman's letters that contained advances. On occasion Hyman was obliged to take action against an agent who failed to fulfill his agreement and simply pocketed the money Hyman sent him. The following is an excerpt from a letter to Moïse Bernier of L'Islet, dated 20 August 1867:

> Not only have you injured and deceived me like a dishonest man as you are by Pocketing the £10 I sent you which you pretended it was to give to the fishermen which you never hired, but you must insult me yet -- I have already written to Charles Hamilton Esqr. Québec, who will find you if you are any way above ground or a Rag to get hold of ...[64]

William Hyman preferred to hire the same men year after year; this is why he often made arrangements at the close of the fishing season. It was, however, rare for a man to work for him more than two years running; the "Canadiens" moved around a great deal. Lepage[65] mentions this with reference to Percé. There was undoubtedly competition among agents in the various localities, and some of the men might well have tried working in several Gaspé fishing establishments. As mentioned earlier, many inhabitants of the various parishes immigrated to the north shore of the St. Lawrence, or to the United States to work in the factories. Fishermen and shoremen, unlike splitters and salters, were poorly paid. Table 6 shows that wages remained virtually constant over a 35-year period.

As mentioned earlier, at the beginning of the 19th century it was very difficult for a beach master to transfer an employee to a job other than the one for which the man was hired at the beginning of the season. Around mid-century, employees appear to have been very mobile and were constantly being shifted from one job to another according to the merchant's requirements. At the end of the season, when ships were being loaded at Gaspé, Hyman sent a couple of "Canadiens" to work for the captain.[66] He was also known to fire or replace an employee for reasons not necessarily related to productivity: "I discharged a smart boy a Canadian for his saucy tongue but other wise he is a smart working man ..."[67] Fishing and processing at large company fishing establish-

Table 6.   Monthly wages of William Hyman and Sons' employees, 1857-93.[a]

Year	Fisherman	Shoreman	Salter	Splitter	Cook	Farmer
1857	75/ [b]			110/		
1859	60/ - 90/	60/ - 65/	65/ - 95/			
1860	75/ - 90/	50/ - 62/6	110/		60/	
1861	80/ - 100/	50/ - 65/	90/		45/	
1862	40/	60/				
1863		50/ - 57/	80/			57/
1864		60/ - 65/	100/	75/	65/	
1865		42/ - 65/		140/-145/	55/	
1866		50/ - 60/	100/	140/	55/	
1867	50/	40/ - 60/	100/		60/	
1868		55/				
1872		$13 - $15,50			$12	$12 - $15
1873		$13 - $16			$12	$18
1874		$13 - $17		$20	$10	$16
1875		$12 - $18	$20	$30	$6 - $12	$14
1877		$10 - $15				
1878		$11 - $14	$22			
1879		$10 - $12	$22			
1880		$9 - $12	$22		$8	
1881		$12			$12	
1882		$9				
1883		$11 - $12			$12	
1885		$8 - $14				
1886		$8 - $10,50				
1893		$12 - $14				

[a]Eleven of the thirty-six years are missing because the ledgers for those years do not list men by trade. We have included wages only for men whose trades are clearly specified; the table is a record of changes in wages according to trade. Figure 14 provides more precise numbers of employees.

[b]20/ = 20 shillings = £ sterling = $4.00.

ments and company beaches was done by seasonal workers. The workers included fishermen, splitters, salters and shoremen, and, as the men lived onsite, a cook, also hired each summer. Many men were hired by Hyman to work on independent beaches; the planters paid Hyman for the expenses incurred. We have referred to the strategy governing use of these men's services and to the factors that influenced their number. We shall return to the subject later and to the conditions under which "Canadiens" were hired.

Production Units

When we have made the social distinctions between the shoremen, the fishermen and the seasonal workers, we have also mentioned their place of work; these could be indentified as production units, thus indicating the aspects of the social and geographical distribution of the fishing organisation. As we have seen, there were two distinct aspects of production -- fishing and processing. The operations were not performed by the same men but were always linked to a specific fishing room. Fishermen who set out from a given beach returned to it with their catch, which was then processed. In the Gaspé context, "the fishing room" was not only a beach, but the entire production infrastructure, including all equipment, buildings, and men required to produce dried cod. The room was the framework, the unit of production and, because our point of reference is the finished product (dried cod), it includes both fishermen and shoremen. As production involved two main operations, it required two work units, fishermen and shoremen. It would be even more accurate to speak of a work unit for each operation, each unit working in a specific location. According to the detailed description given by Captain Fortin in 1859 (Rapports Fortin 1859), work units were distributed as shown in Table 7. To the specialized duties in Table 7

Table 7.   Division of labour in a Gaspé company beach establishment in the mid-19th century.

Operation	Work Unit	Title	Location
		Catch and Processing	
fishing	fishermen	fishing master, helper	boat
splitting	dressers	throater, header, splitter	splitting table (splitting cabin on stage head)
salting	salters	salter, kencher	stage
washing	washers	washer	trough outside stage or in nearby building
kenching	kenchers	kencher	stage
drying	shoremen	beach master, shoremen	flakes, beach, storehouses
		Fish Handling	
unloading boats	fishermen	fishing master, helper	stage head
transport of fish to splitting table	cabin boys	cabin boys	stage head to splitting cabin
transport of split fish to salting	cabin boys	cabin boys	from stage head to flakes
transport from salting to washing	cabin boys	cabin boys	stage to annex

should be added end-of-season weighing under the direction of the culler, who also assessed product quality and casking, or packing cod into barrels for shipment. These are not included in the table because they are related to the finished product.

Company Establishments

The description given by Fortin corresponds to the organization of labour at a large company fishing establishment, the type of organization we should expect to find at Grande-Grave, for example, the Fruing or Hyman company. Fortin says he is describing a typical Gaspé coast fishing establishment, allowing for variation between individual establishments (equipment, location of operations, allocation of duties). There was no variation in the operations as such; every establishment used the same technical process to obtain the same end product. The labour force at the William Hyman company was almost exclusively made up of seasonal workers, that is, "Canadiens." The only local people employed were the beach master, who acted as foreman, and skilled

19. Flakes and warehouses on the Fruing company beach, ca. 1900; at far right on a plateau is Hyman establishment.

workers, for example, blacksmith, carpenter, cooper and farmer. We
have restricted our description to the production area of a company
beach establishment; Appendix H shows that there were also living areas
for servants, other employees and managers, administrative and business
areas and an agricultural area.

Independent Fishing Rooms

The fishing rooms belonging to the planters were similar to large
fishing establishments, but on a smaller scale and without any business
area; although some planters did distribute goods such as flour. There
were, however, differences between independent and company establishments in three areas: equipment, salting and labour force. According to
descriptions and iconographic documents, an independent plant had no
stage head; splitting was done on the beach. Stages required a great deal
of space, and the labour and materials required to build a stage at the
beginning of every season and tear it down at the end would increase
production costs. The company establishments salted by kench cure, the
planters by pickle cure, that is, by piling sliced cod in barrels with salt
between each layer, thus soaking the cod in brine. Apparently the

20. Beach master Simon's family establishment at Anse-aux-Sauvages, ca. 1885.

merchants tried unsuccesfully to persuade the producers to abandon the pickle cure, as kenching was thought to give a superior finished product. It is difficult to know whether or not this was the case, or merely a plea by European intermediates when they were having trouble getting a good price for cod on the European market.[68]

The labour force at an independent plant was made up of both seasonal workers and members of the family unit, that is, the planter's immediate family and relatives. In our earlier assessment of the labour force, we saw that the structure of the fishing industry was based on large company establishments and independent plants, both staffed partly by the annual influx of a seasonal labour force of "Canadiens." At the beginning of the 19th century local fishermen worked mostly at large company establishments, either as company employees or as beach masters. By mid-century this was still the case, but now, partly because of an increase in population, more and more production was carried out on small satellite rooms. The multiplication of these small establishments, due to population increases, subdivision of land and population spread, paralleled the gradual disappearance of the labour force of "Canadiens." From a structure based mainly on large establishments and a migrant labour force, we see a gradual change to a structure based on large establishments increasingly staffed by a local land-poor labour force, and increasingly dependent on small independent rooms staffed almost exclusively by members of family units. The main observable factor causing change in the 19th century is the rise of these small independent fishing rooms. This phenomenon, which was accompanied by a territorial expansion of the companies and their clientele, probably restricted the adaptability of Gaspé merchant capital. The spread of production over a larger area was bound to lead to problems in product uniformity, and the increased demand for credit necessarily placed restrictions on the companies, who were then faced with three possibilities. They were obliged either to restrict the number of dealers and operate within their former limits, attempt to expand with the ensuing risk of control and profitability problems, or limit credit and so lessen control over their producers and risk losing them to competitors.

Statistical records on the labour force in Gaspé make no mention of the importance of the family unit; each statistical category includes only fishermen and shoremen. We have no way of knowing whether "shoremen" include both migrant workers and members of family units or migrant workers only. In addition, the statistics refer to a location or group of locations and make no distinction between large and small establishments. Nevertheless, two things were likely constant in the independent rooms. First, as in company establishments there was a strict division of labour between fishermen and shoremen; second, within a family unit, fishermen heads of families did the shorework (splitting and salting) after the day's fishing, the drying being supervised by the women. Data on the beginning of the 20th century indicate that this was the common practice.[69] In the mid-19th century there is no clear-cut evidence that this was the case among local fishermen but the diversity of Hyman's dealers suggests it. Several producers appear to have been truly independent, that is, not associated with a planter. There were also many partnerships where two fishermen shared a room.

Schooners

If a unit of production is defined with reference to the entire process that produced dried cod, a schooner cannot be considered a unit of production. These vessels were not, however, merely fishing boats; splitting and salting were done on board. The fish were dried on a Gaspé beach at the end of each fishing trip. According to William Hyman's correspondence, his schooners delivered draft cod to his beach.[70] As we saw in the section on types of fishing, a schooner's crew often formed a club of five or six men. Schooners and sailors were recorded in the fisheries statistics as categories separate from fishing boats, fishermen and shoremen. The labour force involved in this type of fishing was linked not to a plant but to the schooner.

This examination of the production process has resulted in a rather lengthy report because it was necessary to examine each aspect of the process in logical order. By specifying at the start the limitations inherent in fishing, we were able to establish the operating limits as they affected both product and work methods, at the same time defining the parameters affecting production level. Analysis of the operations involved in production, and of the skills required of the labour force, points out the technical basis of the coastal fishery with reference to the resource, the equipment and the producers. The chapter ends with the classification of units of production in order to better understand the system's adaptability and to open the way for a more qualitative analysis of the social aspects.

III PRODUCTION OF DRIED COD -- SOCIAL ASPECTS

Relationships Between Fishermen and Merchants

The ledgers of merchants and merchants' companies provide detailed economic data on the situation of hundreds of people. Behind the multiplicity and the complexity of the transactions recorded in those ledgers, one can detect the web of the relationships between the fishermen and the merchants. A study of the ledgers dispels the myths surrounding the stereotypical Gaspé fisherman. The accounts reveal a wide variety of interaction among a merchant's dealers. In addition to the unilateral fisherman-dealer/merchant relationship, these volumes depict interaction between fishermen-dealers and between dealers and non-dealers. They reflect each fisherman's consumption (debit) and production (credit), habits and, in transfers between accounts, the exchange of services between fishermen. The ledger, then, is the record of all financial transactions involving all dealers and depicts various types of interaction and co-operation among fishermen.

A fisherman's account, a record of a purely economic link with a company, is a source of information not only on production, but on family relationships, inheritance practices, real estate transactions, religious duties (tithing), legal transactions, distribution of consumer goods (for example, flour, potatoes) and exchange of services (work of skilled craftsmen). The buying of goods provides information on their production methods (nets, salt, gear), diet, household tasks (construction, dressmaking, etc.), alcohol consumption, marriage customs (purchase of wedding rings), births, hunting, trapping, etc. The information recorded in the accounts indicates a man's relationship with a company allowed a merchant to know many aspects of a fisherman's daily life. The very word "company" had connotations far wider than that of an economic agent. There is no one word that includes all the implications of the terms "merchant" and "bourgeois" as used by fishermen speaking of the company. A company encompassed a vast network of relations; it was viable because of the fishermen's accounts, and the merchants' influence at all levels of the political and legal establishment. These social and economic bodies could more accurately be called "houses" and indeed, observers often referred to the Robin company as the "maison Robin" (House of Robin). Although it is not our intention here to elaborate on the analytical implications of such a concept, the current notion of "company" is far narrower that it was in 19th century Gaspé.

Ledgers

All transactions between the Hyman company and its dealers were recorded in two volumes: the day book and the ledger. The former was a day-to-day record of all transactions with dealers. These were subsequently entered in each fisherman's personal account in the ledger. The ledger provides a complete record of every dealer's transactions; it contains personal, dated, double-entry accounts -- debits on the left-hand page, credits on the right; it also contains an index of names. One volume usually covers one or two years for a specific fishing establishment (Grande-Grave, Rivière-au-Renard, Cap-des-Rosiers, etc.). Local producers' accounts were usually opened in January and closed in December, and the balance (positive or negative) carried over each year. The ledger provides a permanent record of each dealer's transactions; the cross-referencing facilitates reconstruction of each man's life.

The Hyman company also kept private ledgers, fish books, order books, invoice books, sundries accounts, flour books and log books.

The private ledgers are a record of all transactions related to supply of and production by every company fishing station and vessel. They follow the same double-entry method as the accounts of individual producers, each fishing station being treated as a company dealer. The books mentioned in the preceding paragraph contain a variety of specific operations related to the normal running of a company. The third most important books -- after ledgers and private ledgers -- are the letter-books, which contain all correspondence dealing with management of the company and each of its establishments. This correspondence, as mentioned earlier often clarifies items in the ledgers and other records and, more importantly, relates the merchant's local activity to the structure of international trade.

The Fisherman as Dealer

In 19th century Gaspé, the fishery operated within a unique trade structure in which fishermen were considered dealers. The concept of "fisherman-dealer" refers to the way the fisherman fits into the commercial fishing structure. It includes the fisherman's utter dependence on the merchant both for acquiring his means of production and disposing of his production. To the merchant, a fisherman was above all a dealer, a supplier of dried cod. Credit was the moving force behind all production. It was the bond that underlay all production-related agreements. The merchant advanced the means of production to the dealer; the dealer delivered the product. Advances, or credit, were what made production possible. Without credit there was no production, at least not on the scale seen in Gaspé at that time.

We have seen to what extent a company intervened in the fishermen's lives. Obviously some aspects of a fisherman's life were unrelated to production, and so were not subject to merchant control. Even when it came to production, a fisherman was not necessarily restricted to dealing with one company; some fishermen undoubtedly dealt with two or more. There are several instances of a fisherman transferring his account from Hyman to Fruing; Hyman's correspondence contains several passages accusing Fruing of "stealing" his dealers.

Within the specific context of the dealer-company relationship, implying as it does advances given to a fisherman by a company, it seems illogical that a fisherman would deliver part of his production to one company and the rest to another, which had presumably provided him with advances as well. Such a dealer would be considered unsteady by the companies. For example, if at the end of a season, the second company were to offer a higher price for fish than the first (as sometimes happened), the fisherman could repay the advances given him by the first company with his profit from the second, or simply have his first account bought out by the second. There is little evidence of such practices in the accounts. When times were good and competition heavy, the number of fishermen who changed company probably increased.

Table 8 shows that of our 1860 sample of Hyman dealers, only 13 percent delivered their total annual cod production to the company. This figure was arrived at by comparing the number of quintals of cod delivered to Hyman (as recorded in the fishermen's accounts for 1860) with the number of quintals declared by the fishermen the following winter at the time of the 1861 census. This 13 percent of "loyal"

Table 8. Distribution of producers according to the proportion of their cod production delivered to William Hyman in 1860.[a]

No. producers	% production delivered	No. quintals	% total received
15	0-9	106	4
9	10-19	80	3
7	20-29	148	5
10	30-39	200	7
6	40-49	148	5
7	50-59	303	10
9	60-69	407	14
5	70-79	251	9
3	80-89	146	5
2	90-99	135	5
11	100	956	33
84[b]		2880	100

[a]The proportion of quintals delivered to the company is established on the basis of production declared to the census taker for the 1860 fishing season.

[b]Not equal to total number of producers in Table 9 because (1) several of Hyman's dealers were not included in the census taker's lists, (2) several dealers who delivered fish to Hyman did not declare the amounts to the census taker, and (3) very small accounts (those overdue by a few quintals of cod) are not included.

producers provided 33 percent of Hyman's total production. The figures reflect the concentration of production in establishments run by independent planters. Hyman's own fishing establishment accounted for 6 percent of total production, therefore Hyman controlled approximately 40 percent of total production. In addition, 44 percent of his dealers delivered more than half their individual production to him. As these dealers accounted for 76 percent of Hyman's total production, his control over them was considerable.

Table 9 gives the 1860 breakdown of dealers with William Hyman and shows that the structure of company production was based on roughly two major types of dealers: a large number of dealers who had a small production, and a small number of dealers who had a large production. Each group accounted for about 50 percent of production, but the large dealers were undoubtedly more easily controlled. The distribution of William Hyman's dealers seems to reflect a transition period in which a production structure inherited from the late 18th century was in conflict with population growth since that time. The traditional structure (merchant, planter, fisherman, seasonal worker), based on a concentration of production in a limited number of locations,

Table 9.   William Hyman and Sons' producer categories in 1860.

Category	No. producers	Production in quintals	% of total production
Independent dealers	148	2850	49
Merchants	3	1301	22
Planters	9	1023	18
Salaried workers	(21) [a]	346 [b]	6
Schooners	2	276	5
Total	162 (183)	5796	100

[a] This includes fishermen and shoremen.

[b] This is the difference between number of quintals exported according to the Gaspé harbour record and the number of quintals delivered according to the records in the fishermen's accounts. As the Hyman's beach production came from wage workers with no production reference in their account, we presume here that their share of the production is included in this difference.

was changing at the same time as the upsurge of production by smaller units managed by a larger number of producers working outside the traditional structure.

Table 10 shows that William Hyman's dealers were located mainly in Cap-des-Rosiers and Douglas townships. The company did have dealers in all the surrounding townships, but the producer-dealers were concentrated in these two. Table 11 shows that almost 80 percent of the Cap-des-Rosiers township family heads were Hyman's dealers. The low

Table 10. Number of heads of families in each township dealing with the Hyman company in 1861.

Mont-Louis	3
Rivière-au-Renard	17
Cap-des-Rosiers	124
Gaspé Bay north	48
Gaspé Bay south	27
North Sydenham	3
South Sydenham	9
York	6
Douglas	108
Malbaie	15
Percé	4
Total[a]	364

[a]Producers and non-producers.

Table 11. Heads of families who dealt with Hyman in 1861 for each locality in Cap-des-Rosiers township.

Anse-au-Griffon	15	out of	36	(42%)
Jersey Cove	6	out of	8	(75%)
Cap-des-Rosiers	51	out of	56	(91%)
Shiphead	10	out of	10	(100%)
Anse-aux-Sauvages &Cap-aux-Os	15	out of	15	(100%)
Petit-Gaspé	12	out of	16	(75%)
Grande-Grave	11	out of	11	(100%)
Anse-St-Georges	4	out of	4	(100%)
Total	124		156	(79%)

proportion of dealers in Anse-au-Griffon was due to the presence of John Le Boutillier's company. The 1861 census shows that the important planters of Grande-Grave, Anse-St-Georges and Anse-aux-Sauvages delivered only a small part of their production to Hyman, the greater part of their production being delivered to Hyman's main competitor, the Fruing company.

The wide variation in the extent to which Forillon heads of families were obligated to William Hyman raises the question of the degree of dependence included in the dealer-company relationship. Many Hyman company dealers traded only part of total production, that is, delivered only part of their fish, to Hyman. The dealer-merchant relationship with Hyman represented only part of their activities as producers and consumers, and so their accounts reflect only part of their activity as producers and in these cases the company ledgers reveal only a fragmentary picture of their social and economic life. Obviously business and trading were not a fisherman's whole life. If the dealer-merchant relationship was in actual fact crucial in determining how fishermen earned their living, it might have influenced other relations as well. Marriages, for example, could have been contracted for the purpose of retaining a favourable trade position. A planter who had no sons might well try to choose potentially good producers as husbands for his daughters. Inheritance practices were probably influenced by the extent of a producer's obligation to the company; for if a debt was large enough, the company would be able to seize his room when he died. There are many indications that such considerations existed. The problem of reconciling a producer's total activity as producer with his activity as dealer with a given company is only a matter of degree. Some producers may have managed to escape total control by the local company, but at the regional level there was no way to avoid trading with a company. On the Gaspé Peninsula, where production was initiated and supported by credit in the form of company advances to fishermen, each fisherman's production eventually reached a company storehouse. Examination of an individual fisherman's account with a given company may be insufficient to establish his total dependence on that company; if all ledgers of all companies were available, a general picture of a relationship based on the fishermen's dependence on the companies would undoubtedly emerge. Tables 8 and 9 illustrate this kind of relationship in the case of William Hyman's dealers who dealt only with him. The most that can be gathered from differences in the dealers' level of dealing to a given company is that producers dealt with several competing companies. If a fisherman was only half loyal to one company, it means only that the other half of his loyalty was with another company.

Almost all Forillon heads of families dealt with William Hyman, but to differing degrees. These differences give a better perspective on the company's control over producers. By analyzing regular producers we obtain a picture of actual company control, and the conditions under which that control was maintained. By analyzing less dependent producers in the light of changing conditions, we can see why some of them eventually came under greater company control. As an example, one of Hyman's small producer-dealers suddenly begins getting large advances and delivering a greater proportion, or all, of his production to

Hyman. If we are to grasp all the aspects of merchant control and the limits of its flexibility, we need to know the reasons for such a change, and how to spot any possible clues that it was imminent.

The dealer concept lends itself to a study of all possible relations within the trading system as it existed in Gaspé. A company's dealer network covered a far larger area than the locality or village at the time. The possibility of extending the network was directly related to the companies' ability to extend credit. Over and above ethnic and religious differences, which have been the source of problems in other parts of Quebec, residents of Gaspé seem to have found a bond in their mutual dependence on the trading system and the fact that they were both part and victim of it. The dealer concept provided regional identity, reflected the social distinctions between fishermen and was the basis of the hierarchical structure of a company's dealer network.

The Credit System

At first glance, the credit system appears simple. Merchants made annual advances of money and goods to dealers; dealers delivered fish and performed work in repayment. Advances were most numerous in spring when fishermen were preparing for the fishing season; repayments were highest at the end of the season when the fishermen's production was finished. However, social and economic conditions complicate the study of the application of the credit system. On what basis, for example, did a company grant advances? To receive advances a man had to provide several guarantees, but the records provide little information on either the guarantees themselves or the methods used by the merchants to assess them. The only way in which we can establish any basis for assessing a dealer's solvency is by researching his social and economic position for demographic (family) and real estate data. A fisherman's account is a record of his performance as consumer and producer; nowhere is there any question of ability. Obviously a fisherman-dealer's solvency depended on his ability to produce. This ability included skill, ownership of a beach and ability to mobilize a labour force. Advances were an investment in production and never given lightly. This is why advances implied fairly strict control over producers.

Generally speaking, the system of advances was the root cause of producer indebtedness because the value of a fisherman's annual production never equalled the value of his annual advances. When a fisherman's account was closed at the end of the year, there was nearly always a negative balance to be carried forward into his account for the coming year. A producer's account was, in fact, always open and stayed that way as long as he continued to produce dried cod. Because his account was constantly overdue, the fisherman was in a very poor position with respect to the merchant who gave him credit. Settlement could be demanded at any time; if times were hard (poor fishing season, loss of a boat, unavailability of labour) a debt was a powerful tool which the

21. Gaspé store of William Hyman and Sons at the beginning of the 20th century.

merchant could use as evidence to seize goods and property. In Gaspé, debt was a result of the credit system. It was the most important factor in controlling the producers.

The credit system used in Gaspé has frequently been equated with the truck system. This misconception has been, and still is, believed by many people, Gaspé residents and researchers alike. Popular opinion sees the honest fisherman trading his catch for goods in a company store, say a quintal of cod for a barrel of flour, and going home happy to be providing for his family. This image of the fishermen in no way reflects the real pressures faced by them. A truck system is an equal exchange between partners, but examination of the fishermen's accounts indicates rather repayment of a debt owed by the fisherman to the merchant or company that advanced his means of production. The fishermen were not free to trade their catch as they saw fit; the merchant had prior rights to it. A truck system might very well have been used by the fishermen themselves, for example, exchange of farm products for fish, a given amount of work, a specific service, etc. The tithe was sometimes paid in fish, but it was current practice for it to be taken directly out of a Catholic fisherman's account.

The fisheries historian Harold Innis refers to the truck "system," but on elaboration it is the credit system he is actually describing. To pretend that the system was a truck system served an ideological function because it presented the trading method in a positive light and successfully hid the underlying negative aspect of dependence. The equal partner pretence does have some basis in fact in that fishermen and merchants did have mutual obligations, without which the trading system would have collapsed. We will discuss this further later.

The reader will perhaps have a better grasp of the scope of the credit system if we list all the classes of goods and services included under the heading of "advances." We will also list the categories of products provided by the fisherman (fish, work) in repayment of his account. In order of importance (in both value and proportion of the total account) the first debit item is means of production, that is, salt, fishing gear, tackle and equipment required for processing; these were the actual "advances" (the ones we later call advances for production) that is, the means supplied by the merchant before the fishing season. The most expensive of these were salt and nets. The second item was food, the most expensive being flour and meat (barrels of pork, etc.). Next are clothing, mostly yard goods, footwear, protective clothing for fishing and winter clothing. Following that are hardware and building materials (tools, nails, lumber, guns, gunpowder, etc.). Last on the debit list are items of household equipment (stoves, furniture, etc.). There is the occasional carriage or sleigh and, among the young fishermen, wedding rings were common items. There were also miscellaneous transactions, which varied widely from one fisherman to another and from year to year. These included all manner of payments to persons whose names were recorded in the account, generally wages paid to servants and small sums paid to a variety of persons. These categories include most credit purchases. They do not include the entire account; there were always extraordinary payments outside the usual categories. The largest of these was always the debt carried forward from the preceding year. There were also various debts and interest payments, and amounts related to real estate transactions.

The most important item on the credit page is fish delivered by the fisherman, dried, salted or green. Next are various payments by other persons or companies to the fisherman, wages for work done on a daily, weekly or monthly basis, the occasional sale of an animal (steer, calf, sheep, horse), cash payments made by the fisherman or some other person, on rare occasions a boat or flat and oars provided by a boat builder and, often, goods returned to the company store.

Most advances were made in the spring and fall, especially the former. Although it is impossible to verify every case, it seems that fall advances were based on production during the summer season; the size of an individual's advance depended on his performance during the summer. New advances were sometimes made on the day following a fisherman's last summer delivery. It is easy to distinguish summer and fall deliveries -- the first began in mid-August, the second in mid-October. There is, however, no clear-cut distinction between spring advances and fall advances except where it is known that a man did produce a fall catch.

To understand all the implications of the credit system it is necessary to realize that its viability on a local scale depended on its inclusion in a broader national and international credit system. William Hyman was known to remind impatient suppliers of the restrictions inherent in the operation of three interlocking systems: "... as our trade here is entirely on credit, and cannot be realised before a twelve month, you ought to extend your credit to six month..."[1]

Local credit was granted on a short-term basis, usually for four or five months. The fishermen received the largest advances in May and their first deliveries of fish were done in mid-August; summer fish was delivered through September, fall fish until November. Nationally (in Gaspé, Halifax, Quebec City and Montreal), credit was medium-term, that is, between six and twelve months. Hyman usually placed his large orders with merchants in these locations twice a year, in early spring and early fall. Internationally, credit was granted for longer terms (twelve months or more). During the winter, Hyman received advances from his creditors in Europe for the shipments beginning to arrive in southern Europe and South America; these were not repaid until his agents realized the profits of these shipments during the following summer and fall. The annual advances from European financiers and agents (wholesalers) were used by Hyman to order goods in Europe, Quebec City and Montreal, goods which he in turn advanced to his producers. This was the credit cycle, and obviously any delay in the arrival of advances from Europe affected short and medium term credit and, inversely, any delay or drop in production affected the entire system. A poor fishing season affected the availability of credit because of poor sales in Europe; poor sales in Europe could just as easily affect the following year's fishing season. On the local and regional level, the total credit available to prepare a given fishing season depended on the preceding season's recorded performance and on European market conditions; local distribution of credit was based on the productivity and solvency of the individual producer. The total credit available did of course influence local distribution, because it made credit more readily available and thus a number of producers could enter the system; when times were hard, tighter credit resulted in more selective distribution of advances to reliable producers.

Obviously the establishment and operation of such a vast credit system involved risks due to real constraints. The greatest was undoubtedly the risk of two or more consecutive poor seasons. Not everyone was affected equally by a poor season. Poor fishing was generally limited to a specific area; Gaspé Bay could have a poor season and Chaleur Bay a good one; on an even smaller scale, fishing could be good at Rivière-au-Renard and poor at Grande-Grave. Fishermen were the first to suffer from poor fishing in their area. A merchant like William Hyman, who had fishing stations spread over a large area, would not be as adversely affected; he would at least have some profit to make up for his losses. The European financiers survived poor seasons in the same way as the merchants, except their capital was more widely distributed and could be invested in other industries in Europe or elsewhere. The trading system certainly could not control the productive capacity of each fishing season; on the international scale there was plenty of leeway for alternative investment.

Within the system itself, movement of the product and other goods also involved risks because of the operating expenses involved. Interest was charged at each step of the system, the first being local distribution of advances. These interest charges appear in the fishermen's accounts as two different prices for goods and product: "cash price," or the price of goods traded for cash outside the credit system and, "trade price" (always higher), the price for goods traded on credit within the system. Generally, the trade price was the price charged in virtually all transactions recorded in the account of a fisherman-dealer as most of these men had credit accounts. There were several "cash accounts," all transactions being strictly for cash. It seems surprising that these accounts are included in the ledgers, until one sees that payment was always deferred. Even within credit accounts some transactions are for cash. These are marked with an X in the Hyman ledgers. Some clients had a choice of manner of payment for a given article. An account that shows a debit for several articles bought for cash will show a corresponding credit for several quintals of cod sold for cash. Some fishermen thus received two prices for their cod -- part of their catch was traded on a credit basis, the rest for cash. The cash amounts entered in the credit and debit columns do not always tally; the debit amount is usually larger. In such cases articles originally entered at the cash price were converted to the trade price at the end of the season, in the following manner: "to difference on 100/3 cash to trade 35/9," meaning that a debit of 35/9 was added to the account, to raise the cash price to the trade price.[2] We do not know why two prices were used in one account. A dealer who had a cash account or carried out many of his transactions for cash was undoubtedly in a better financial position than one who did not, simply because he had some money. One of the best ways of closing an account was to pay the total amount owing in cash. Some producers (who had managed to save a little money) were relatively independent of the company financially and were thus less affected by the credit system.

It is difficult to assess the total amount of cash in circulation in the region in the mid-19th century. Most of it was in the hands of the merchants who sometimes had to pay cash, as advances, for goods or for services. Most fishermen's accounts show occasional advances of small sums of money, undoubtedly for services that required cash payment. A large part of the cash in the hands of the merchants and producers was used to give advances and pay wages to seasonal workers, most of whom were migrants. As we saw in the previous chapter, Hyman sent cash advances to his servants in the Montmagny area through his hiring agent. Contracts related to hiring for establishments in Percé also mention payment of cash advances before the opening of the fishing season.[3]

Cash seems to have been a rare commodity, not only in Gaspé, but in Quebec City as well. The draft was the most usual instrument in circulation at the time, and the overall value of these drafts was probably far higher than the money supply available on the market. The scarcity of money is supported by the fact that William Hyman had a variety of sources of supply, as several of his letters confirm.[4] The scarcity of money in Gaspé, and more especially among Gaspé fishermen, is not directly attributable to the local credit system but rather to the financial structure of credit common to 19th century trading in the West. All production in Gaspé was bound up in a firmly rooted credit system; it is not surprising that the increase in the money supply in circulation that occurred around the turn of the century was not immediately felt in Gaspé. Several Hyman company letters dated around 1920 indicate that some increase in supply was beginning to be felt; the company now preferred to run on cash.[5] Credit continued to be an important factor in trade in Gaspé; the failure of the first fishermen's cooperatives demonstrate the extent to which the custom of dealing for credit was rooted in tradition in some locations. At the turn of the century the scarcity of money in Gaspé[6] and on the north shore of the St. Lawrence was seen as a symbol of dependence and under-development. Many fishermen's tales confirm the scarcity; it was 1920 or 1930 before some of them were paid cash for their fish.[7]

In the 19th century the credit system was so firmly established that it affected not only trade between fishermen and companies, but even trade among fishermen. This suggests that the fishermen's accounts reveal not only the economic aspect of trade between company and fishermen, but important social aspects as well. Many accounts of individual fishermen contain items, in both credit and debit columns, that refer to other fishermen by name. These items show that individuals exchanged money, goods and services through these accounts. An analysis of these transactions reveals the structure of work crews, partnerships, trading networks, etc., based on, for example, family relationship. Obviously trading under the credit system profoundly affected social life and social relationships, even those apparently unrelated to any economic considerations. The extent of merchant control can also be seen by examining real estate transactions in the area (Appendix B). These transactions and the personal relationships between merchants and fishermen will now be examined, as they were applied in the credit system.

Mutual Obligations and the Dynamics of Trade

Harold Innis has written that companies and fishermen both paid a high price for the introduction of the trading system into the cod fishery -- the merchants because of the limitations and fluctuations inherent in the industry, the fishermen because of the heavy burden of living on credit. For their participation in the system, the fishermen were rewarded with debt and the consequent risk of mortgage or seizure of property that could force them out of the local fishing industry altogether. The almost daily entry of transactions in the ledgers gave the merchants a complete record on each fisherman, as well as a knowledge of his credit requirements and his productivity. Each person's debt was closely monitored, and his credit limit was established following an as yet undetermined procedure. One thing is certain -- the merchant was familiar with each fisherman's personal and family life, and this gave him an enormous advantage when it came to strictly personal relations. A merchant rarely had to face any concerted pressure from dealers. The only exception to this occurred following a poor fishing season when dealers could demand, and get in cash, a higher price for their fish. The annual reports of the fishery office contain several references to work stoppages (interpreted as desertion) by fishermen hired by a company; the fishermen in question refused to put out to sea because of extremely poor fishing conditions.

Generally, William Hyman treated each case individually and any pressure he could exert on a fisherman was probably unknown to anyone else. A fisherman's account often contains an acknowledgment of debt. These are notes of hand signed by the fisherman acknowledging his debt to the merchant and undertaking to repay it in three' or four yearly instalments, plus interest. Notes of hand were entered in a fisherman's debit column, but were not included in the total amount of his advances. On receipt of the annual instalment, the merchant deducted the amount from the original debt, and so on until the debt was paid off, if it ever was. Once a note of hand was signed, a new account was then opened. It seems the merchant made a judgment in each case concerning the level at which the debt required an official note of hand. A fisherman sometimes signed an acknowledgment of debt on the page of the ledger. In the course of compiling a systematic list of real estate transactions registered in Percé, we discovered that an acknowledgment of debt always included a legal document, that is, a bond or mortgage. The merchants' advances to the dealers were thus guaranteed by the dealers' real property. Real estate transactions formed an integral part of the dealer-merchant trading pattern; the use of bonds and mortgages to guarantee repayment of advances led to a sharp increase in the volume of legal records concerning real estate. Between 1842 and 1896 more than half the real estate transactions on the Forillon Peninsula involved either the Hyman or the Fruing company.8 Intra-family transactions were few. Our hypothesis is that the companys' powers of expropriation discouraged people from amassing real property or prevented any such property from being transferred internally in the case of fishermen in difficulty. The large number of land transactions at Forillon suggest land speculation, and the value of a lot probably depended more on proximity to a beach and fishing establishment than on size or agricultural potential. The transactions also reveal something of the nature of the fisherman-company relationship. Of the 227 real estate transactions involving the Hyman company between 1842 and 1896, 73 were purchases and 45 sales. There were also 50 bonds signed in Hyman's favour by fishermen, for a total of 168 transactions (74%) involving expropriation and redistribution of lots. These bonds were in fact the legal instrument by which a fisherman acknowledged his debt to the company.

Reading and studying the company ledgers and records of real estate transactions suggest a fisherman-company relationship based on rigid company control and an inflexible trading system. But the fishermen who lived under the system probably did not feel themselves to be its slaves, as most outside observers have depicted them. It is far more likely that trading between fishermen and merchants was subject to the dynamics of a specific social ethic. Despite the extent of merchant control, Gaspé in the 19th century shows no evidence of forced labour. The trading system was of course geared to accumulating the largest possible amount of capital; its profitability was necessarily subject to certain rules of economics. In the fishing industry, profitability also depended on its adaptablility to the social standards of the fishermen. In other words, successful operation of the trading system, like any other economic production system, was conditional on its acceptance by the producers on whom operation was based. The fishermen's debts gave the merchants enormous control over them, but if a merchant wanted to keep his regular dealers, he had to be flexible and not threaten the fishermen unduly. However, competition between merchants was not the only reason for flexibility in trade between fishermen and merchants. If it were, the dynamics of trade would have had a purely economic basis. Far more important than economic considerations was conformity to social standards, which divided the behaviour of a member of the community into two types, one admissible, the other quite inadmissible.

In his remarkable monograph on the Newfoundland village of Cat Harbour,[9] James C. Faris speaks of the existence, in 1964-65, of a trading system comparable to the system that governed the Gaspé fishery a century earlier. This may be a surprise to those accustomed to today's rapid changes in the capitalist system that governs most sectors of production. There are several parts of the world where, at the beginning of the 20th century, industrial capitalism had not yet gained complete control of the fishing industry.[10] Establishment of the 200-mile limit has undoubtedly made total control imminent. In 1965, at the same time as the situation in Cat Harbour was reported, anthropologists working on the north shore of the St. Lawrence[11] observed that the fishery was organized along the lines of the trading system introduced in the mid-19th century. Thus in the 1960s there were still remote areas in Canada where the system inherited from the 19th century remained.

On the basis of his observations at Cat Harbour, Faris described the social ethic we referred to earlier. In Cat Harbour a company controlled the greater part of local production through a system of credit to fishermen, despite the fact that all the fishermen were members of a local fishermen's cooperative. Just as in 19th century Gaspé, the Cat Harbour credit system gave the local merchant great power over the fishermen because of their debts, which represented the fishermen's economic and social obligations to him. Faris states that although the merchant was extremely powerful as a result of the system, the obligation was mutual, resulting as it did from a fusion of social and economic standards, and that the dynamics of trade depend on the transformation of debt into obligation:

> By debt, I mean a liability incurred in receipt of goods or services, carrying the implication of creditor power over the debtor. Obligation, on the other hand, is a liability the settlement of which one is morally bound to pursue.[12]

It seems that to a fisherman, "debt" symbolizes a merchant's power over him, whereas "obligation" symbolizes the fisherman's moral obligation to his creditor. Considering a debt in the strict sense of the word, a merchant can resort to legal means to collect it; an obligation, however, considers such abstract concepts as respect, loyalty and reputation. Based on the social ethic, the merchant risks weakening his power if he pressures a dealer to pay a debt; similarly, if a fisherman violates his obligation, if he fails to show sufficient respect and loyalty to the merchant, his obligation will become a debt, thus unleashing the legal power held by the merchant. The trade ethic is limited by the fisherman's acceptance of his moral obligation to the merchant and the merchant's refusal to exercise a power that is legally his. Faris asked the Cat Harbour merchant whether he had ever used his power to collect a debt; the merchant said he had not, that a debt was always paid, sooner or later. To meet the requirements of this ethic the merchant had to be fairly well off, especially if there were several poor seasons in succession; the fisherman had to keep producing for "his" merchant.

Another aspect of the ethic is the secrecy surrounding a fisherman's debt:

> Private debts cannot be converted into "public debts" for sanctions to insure obligation. Public knowledge (or speculation -- quite often the details of the truth make little difference) can serve as a focus for conversation which forces a delinquent man to pay his debts in certain circumstances, but usually it simply frustrates the debtor.[13]

Where trading between merchant and fishermen is based on a personal relationship, it is subject to the social restriction of secrecy. This secrecy allows the merchant to increase his power by dividing the fishermen's collective debt into smaller individual debts, leaving no room for collusion. To the fisherman, the secret he shared with the merchant perpetuates the illusion of equality among fishermen unaware of the size of one another's debts. Faris demonstrates very subtly how the required practices governing the dynamics of trade between merchant and fisherman spilled over into the relationship between individual fishermen trading services.

Faris's analysis contributes greatly to our understanding of the social aspect of a trading system operating within a community. He shows in concrete terms that the application of an economic system cannot be fully understood unless it is examined in the context of the social standards that govern it; in a way the merchant did exploit the fishermen, but he was considered part of the community. He ran risks when he extended credit, but a debt could be repaid only according to specific rules. Although the majority of the fishermen were dependent on the merchant because they were in his debt, the dependence was not regarded as negative, as long as trading was carried out according to the rules.

Faris's comments give us an insight into the dynamics of social relations in the context of merchant control over Gaspé fishermen in the 19th century. His analysis is not directly applicable to Gaspé, but it facilitates analysis of any economic system subject to both economic and social restrictions. From a strictly economic point of view, the credit systems in Newfoundland and Gaspé are comparable. We do not, however, have any information on a specific social ethic in Gaspé. Faris does say that his 1964 observations in Cat Harbour are the result of a complete reversal in merchant behaviour. The present merchant's father was far less flexible and very cautious in giving advances to fishermen, as he himself always paid his debts on time. However, even if former conditions of trading were more inflexible, it is extremely unlikely that trade did not adhere to some social ethic. Faris says that it was solely because of tradition that the fishermen dealt with the merchant; they felt more at home with the merchant, even if it meant paying a higher price for their goods.

Although Faris's analysis helps us to understand the Gaspé situation, there are differences. The most important is that the Gaspé fisherman's bond was founded on law, which Faris does not mention for Newfoundland. In addition, there was more than one company operating in Gaspé -- competition was unknown to Cat Harbour. Competition between merchants undoubtedly played a part in the evolution of debt from a moral to a legal obligation. The fishermen's accounts show that if a merchant refused a dealer credit, which presumably would have been contrary to the social ethic, or insisted that he pay his debt, the dealer could always obtain credit elsewhere or even sell his account to another company. The ethic must have been somewhat blurred in times of heavy competition and the power of competition must have varied, for companies all had to deal with the same ecological and economic limitations. The loyalty of so many Hyman dealers suggests a certain ethic underlying the dynamics of trade between a merchant and "his" fishermen.

Once the merchant-fisherman relationship is seen as a part of the overall dynamics of trade we can no longer accept the fishermen's "mentality" as the explanation of their dependence on the companies and the longevity of the trading system run by Channel Islanders in Gaspé. The fishermen's social standards could restrict free operation of the trading system and the system had to adapt to the fisherman's rules if it were to make a profit.

Dealer Relations and Production Relations

Because ledgers are accounting records, the various forms of association among fishermen can be deduced merely from the methods used to pay the fishermen. An account can provide the recorded figures of an agreement or partnership entered into for the express purpose of producing dried cod. An agreement between fishermen is suggested by an apparent sharing of the product's value. The dynamics of the personal relations underlying such agreements are lost to us and our only way of obtaining even a glimpse of them is to reconstruct the networks based on demographic data (family relationship, age-group), real estate (location, proximity), and ethnic origin (Canadian, Jersey Islander, Guernsey Islander, Irish). This procedure can help significantly in understanding the formation and dissolution of work teams. Prior knowledge of the agreements possible within the framework of the credit system will facilitate understanding of the importance of the social networks. Results of the analysis of the accounts of fishermen who dealt with William Hyman follow. We have included only cod producers, except for the merchants referred to in a previous chapter.

The dealer relation involved two aspects of production relations: credit and wages. The former affected only local residents, the latter mainly migrants. With the residents, production was assessed by unit, by share or by catch, with a corresponding unit of measurement for each.

Shares and units were measured by the quintal, catch by the draft. The quintal was used to measure a finished product, the draft green or salted fish.

Table 12. Forms of payment to fishermen who dealt with William Hyman and Sons (1854-63).

Payment	Product	Designation	Unit of measure
By the unit	dried cod	merchantable fish	quintal (112 lb.)
By share		inferior fish	
		talqual fish	
By the catch	green fish	green fish	draft (238 lb.)
	salted fish	salted fish	

Delivery of dried cod usually began at the end of the summer; green and salted cod were delivered daily. The majority of the fishermen who dealt with William Hyman between 1854 and 1863 delivered a finished product; Hyman rarely dealt in fish by the draft. Over this ten-year period Hyman dealt with a yearly average of 133 producers at his Grande-Grave establishment alone. Each producer had a personal account, including fishermen who produced fish in association with others. Whether or not a fisherman belonged to a club or partnership for work purposes, he was assessed individually when it came to his credit requirements. This practice must have had its effect on clubs and partnerships, as the merchant undoubtedly had an influence on the choice of members.

In discussing the organizational structure of the fishery, we mentioned that production was centred on the large plants owned by independent beach masters called planters. There was also some question of distribution of advances to fishermen by the planters. If this were the case, planters would have had to keep their own records of advances and receipts. If an individual fisherman obtained his supplies from a planter, there would have been no need for him to have a large personal account with the company. L'Abbé Gingras observed this method of distribution in the Chaleur Bay area (see long quotation in chapter two), and Lepage conducted a study of its implications for Grande-Rivière.14 There is no evidence of the practice as such among William Hyman's dealers. Planters were given large advances of means of production and money, especially the former; except for a little flour, they were not distributors of goods. A planter was a middleman only in the sense that he was a producer who had other producers working with him, sharing his beach and using his production infrastructure. A planter who dealt with Hyman was not responsible for his fishermen as consumers; they all dealt directly with Hyman. The Chaleur Bay planter or outfitter described by Gingras, however, had significant responsibilities and faced ruin if his fishermen were unable to repay the advances he made them.

From the standpoint of credit and within the production structure, a planter provided a guarantee to Hyman for the work of each individual fisherman on his beach. A fisherman who was a planter's partner or employee was given credit by Hyman on the basis of that association. This explains why each fisherman who contributed to the production of fish delivered to Hyman had an open account with him. Except for wage earners, the individual production of a fisherman who participated in the total production of a plant was never included in the number of quintals recorded in the planter's personal account. Each fisherman's production was always recorded individually, even if he participated in the total recorded for the planter. All this suggests that the fisherman's priority was to find himself a plant or a room to fish from (including, in some cases, use of a boat and fishing gear) to be eligible for credit. An independent producer's ownership of his means of production and beach space were sufficient to make him eligible for credit.

The fisherman's personal accounts contain specific references to association. As we have seen, a fisherman's link to a planter can be found in the planter's personal account, in items referring to the production of individual boats, for example. Other indications were listed immediately after the fisherman's name.

The references to place and association were used somewhat erratically. Reassembling a fishing crew solely on the basis of these ledgers' notices can be difficult because of the men's mobility, even during the course of a single fishing season. For example, a fisherman may be listed as "at" a particular plant at the beginning of the season, but further research shows that he did not work for the planter in question during the entire season. The most important aspect of this "labelling" of individuals is that it kept tabs on the migrant workers within the network of local dealers. The merchant had to keep track of his men, and check that his dealers were in fact producing at a plant.

Migrants' accounts clearly indicate whether a man was a partner or an employee; residents' partnerships are usually not indicated unless a planter is one of the partners. Partnerships between independent fishermen can be traced by analysis of the accounts on the basis of the delivery date of a specific number of quintals of cod to Hyman; for example, we may find that two apparently unrelated individuals each delivered thirty quintals of cod on the same date. As the number of quintals recorded was rarely a whole number, dividing the total into eighths of quintals and into pounds reveals that each individual was credited for half of a total delivery. On occasion one partner is credited with a little more than half of the total production, the other with slightly less; in such cases the existence of the partnership can usually be confirmed from other references. Most partnerships were formed for the express purpose of fishing and drying the catch together; the men were equal partners and shared all production on an equal basis. One of the most common forms of payment mentioned in histories of Gaspé is "half-line." Two men who fished together were paid for one-half of their total catch; the other half went to the merchant or planter who gave them the use of the boat and fishing gear. Thus the two fishermen each had a quarter share. This was not a common practice among Hyman dealers, who were true partners; each was credited for half of total production, because they owned their means of production.

Hyman's correspondence shows that he did sometimes pay by the half-line. Planters rarely paid migrant workers by this method; in 1860 there was only one case. A planter sometimes paid a migrant worker on the basis of number of quintals produced; the migrant then paid his helper a wage out of this amount. William Hyman's correspondence reveals that he dealt with fishing masters, that is, fishermen responsible for a boat; these men decided on the method of paying their helpers.

Most of those who worked for wages were migrants. As we have seen, some migrant fishermen were paid by share or draft, but wages were the most common system. Seasonal shore workers (shoremen), including splitters and salters, were always paid a wage. Processing and handling operations performed by the shoremen had no direct impact on production level; the amount of fish processed could not be greater than the amount caught. Because fishing was itself the most important aspect of production, there were doubtless ways of encouraging fishermen to produce more. A merchant could pay his dealers a wage, pay them by the draft or give them a share of the catch, whichever he considered most appropriate to individual skill and productivity. The fishermen saw the various methods of payment in a different light. A wage-earning fisherman could count on his wage as long as his production remained within certain rather vague limits, whereas the amount earned by a fisherman paid by draft or share was directly proportional to his own effort. One good way of maximizing productivity was probably to assign a wage-earning fisherman to work with a share fisherman; the wage earner would model his effort on the effort of his fishing master, but would still be paid his regular salary. If fishing was good, the situation would be to the share fisherman's advantage as well as the merchant's. Different production strategies could be reflected in different pay arrangements. William Hyman's correspondence and the number of fishermen he hired every year suggest that such strategies were in fact used.[15] Strategy would depend not only on the ability of the producers but also on the return of a fishing season. Apparently when fishing was poor, Hyman increased the number of men assigned to draft fishing to try to fill the freighters he had already chartered during the previous winter. Residents were sometimes assigned to draft fishing, especially at the beginning of the season, to ensure rapid start-up of production at the company beach.

Residents were also paid wages, but not on a permanent basis. Migrants were paid by the month, residents by the day. There were some residents paid by the month, mostly clerks, farmers, craftsmen, shoremen and, rarely, fishermen. Most work for wages was done in the fall at the company beach during the final drying of fish before shipment. Fishermen were put to work for wages drying and handling fish at Grande-Grave and loading at the port of Gaspé. Government projects provided work for many fishermen, especially in the hard times that resulted from successive poor seasons. In the fall of 1868, for example, ten fishermen who dealt with Hyman earned the equivalent of one month's wages for work carried out on the road from Grande-Grave to Cap-des-Rosiers.[16]

The proportion of a fisherman's account made up of credit for wages was highly variable and it did not follow any observable pattern, either from person to person or from year to year. Wages were an "extra" and represented only a small fraction of any one person's total pay. It is difficult to judge the extent to which a merchant could pressure a fisherman to take on a salaried job to reduce a sizeable debt. It seems that the same men were always hired as wage earners, the choice being based on proximity to the fishing establishment and ability. Fish of course made up the major portion of a fisherman's production; other transactions recorded in the fisherman's accounts usually involve building a boat or selling a steer. We came across several such transactions to a value of £8 or £10; for some fishermen, this represents almost one-quarter of their total credit. Unless a dealer had a large enough herd to allow him to sell an animal now and then (unlikely in the case of a steer), he sometimes had no choice but to get rid of an animal to reduce his debt. Boat building is listed so rarely in the accounts that it is difficult to tell whether an order for a boat was given to allow a man to reduce a debt, or was simply an order to a boat builder.

Thus fishing was the primary method by which residents earned their living in the 19th century, and there is no mention whatever in Hyman's ledgers for that period that suggests any upsurge in wages as a means of paying fishermen. Starting around 1870, there is a greater incidence of draft fishing. In the 1850s and 1860s, payment by draft was rare among Hyman dealers. It was also rare for a local fisherman to produce green or salted fish; they dealt in a finished product. But beginning in 1870 we see regular draft fishing by a fair number of residents. For now we can only summarize the factors that brought about the change. First, by the 1880s the wave of migrant workers was receding at the Hyman company, as it was in all of Gaspé. This labour force, which had played such an important part in production strategy, had to be replaced by local labour. Second, the area's increase in population during the 19th century must have filled all available beach space in the area, with the result that many fishermen now owned neither beach nor means of production. Finally, the financial crisis that hit the Gaspé fishery in 1873 had a direct impact on availability of credit to fishing companies. Possibly Hyman became more selective about granting credit. All these factors, in conjunction with the producers' position on the first rung of the production ladder, made them the most vulnerable to change, and left many with nothing to offer but their labour if they wished to remain Gaspé fishermen. Draft fishing gave fishermen the illusion of independence, as they did not work for wages. Production still depended on a man's individual effort, even if he did have to borrow the means of production.

Production relations can be analyzed if one is familiar with the company accounting system. The ledgers have been extremely informative, for behind the dry records lie the relationships, associations, partnerships and agreements that formed the basis of production relations in the industry. The accounting system was vital to the application of a credit system based on a personal relationship between fisherman and merchant; it served as both record and blueprint. The framework within which trading and other transactions were carried out makes an understanding of the dealer-merchant relationship prerequisite to a true understanding of the fishermen's lives. This facet of the relationship also emerged: even strictly economic matters cannot be understood outside the overall social framework. Faris's observations on Cat Harbour have shown how, in Gaspé, economic practices might have influenced social behaviour and formed the basis of a social ethic.

Due to the complete lack of information in historical records concerning the dynamics of personal relations, production relations as seen in the fishermen's personal accounts have been used to establish the economic bases that underlay personal relationships and also restricted them. The main aspects of production relations used as part of the Hyman strategy to increase production were to give credit to local fishermen and to pay wages to migrant workers. Production relations involved a hierarchy in which a planter was a middleman between fisherman and company; the fact that the fishermen were included in the ledgers has been instrumental in uncovering the framework of the organization of labour. Our study has confirmed that catching and processing cod were the primary occupations of fishermen-dealers. The last chapter explains why the production process remained unchanged so long and explores the key role of the fishermen's indebtedness.

IV FISHERMEN IN DEBT

In reconstituting the production process for dried cod we have described the conditions under which it began and how it endured. Production in Gaspé could not be solidly established without considering certain physical, social and economic constraints which must have been a challenge to a system's ability to adapt -- in this case a system of commercial exploitation. In all maritime areas in the world physical constraints, such as the hurricane season in the Gulf of Mexico or the hardship of winter in the Gulf of St. Lawrence, direct and limit fishermen's activity, giving rise to different forms of production organization. Maritime people have to adapt and diversify their strategies, for example, fishing several species simultaneously (or one after another), or simply participating in work processes other than fishing. In areas with similar physical, climatic or maritime conditions, adaptive responses may vary: they are not conditioned strictly by the physical milieu but also by social factors (economic or ideological). Dietary rules, for instance, illustrate how ideology interferes with the use of resources. Because a particular species abounds in one area doesn't automatically mean it will be exploited.

The history of the Gaspé fishing industry gives us a remarkable example of how local producers selected from their resources. Until the 20th century only cod was systematically exploited on a large scale. Aside from being used as bait and fertilizer, herring, capelin, mackerel, squid, cockles, tuna etc. were never fished for commercial purposes. Only a few families regularly hunted whales in the Gaspé Bay, and this was a very specialized activity.[1] For more than a century Americans fished for mackerel around Labrador, Gaspé and the Magdalen Islands, but local fishermen never adopted the practice. Every year in his report the fishery officer deplored the fact that our entrepreneurs and fishermen took no interest in mackerel fishing, which was very lucrative for the Americans.[2] Why, then, only cod? The first two chapters described how Jersey merchants took over the Gaspé and how the exploitation of cod was not only a local adaptive response but mostly a response to market needs. Cod was an abundant resource for which there was a demand and a ready market.

The manner in which cod production was organized in the Gaspé was an adaptive response to, or rather an insertion into, a market governed by a particular commercial system. Because production was initiated by merchants, its social aspects were shaped by the impetus of merchant capital. Relations of production were thus strongly influenced initially by capital imperatives. Credit was used to initiate production, and the resulting debt constituted an efficient instrument for reproduction of long-term social aspects of production and for increasing production. Another way of organizing it would be rigorous state intervention, which fishery officers were calling for and which could have substantially altered the relations of production, as was the case in the United States. If the government had given substantial bounties for fish or helped in building boats, ports and warehouses, Gaspé fishermen might have been encouraged earlier to do offshore or deep-sea fishing, or to diversify their fishing. But state intervention in the Gaspé came late, and only recently as a regular policy.

Fishermen found themselves in debt from beginning to end of their production: they went into debt in order to produce, and because variations in production did not adequately meet their constant and growing consumer needs in order to subsist, production conditions simply perpetuated and increased their initial debt. Debt became general and self-perpetuating in two ways: as the population grew, so inevitably did the social debt, and this debt was transmitted from generation to generation. It grew both in space and time -- in space through the growth in population, and in time through the biological reproduction of the work force. Biological reproduction guaranteed the loyalty of certain families within the merchants' clientele, and population growth ensured the expansion of their business: it allowed them to set up many new fishing ports all over the area. From this model we can judge the conditions under which the Hyman company persevered and expanded. Starting in 1845 with a single base of operations at Grande-Grave, its founder had successfully accumulated many securities in the form of establishments, investments and mortgages.3 The increase in fishermen's social debt went hand in hand with the increase in merchants' wealth.

As mentioned earlier, this indebtedness could be used as a means of control for the merchant and an obligation for the fishermen to produce. Debt remained the main concern within the credit system, as it affected not only the producers but also the merchant. William Hyman also had to give guarantees to his European creditors in difficult times. The social ethic that bound merchant and fishermen together had its equivalent in the international merchant system, and Hyman's voluminous correspondence shows to what extent his credibility had to be upheld by a network of close communications. Being controlled himself, he was obliged to maintain instruments of control over his debtors.

The fisherman's account with the merchant indicated how individual debts evolved. At the end of every year Hyman listed on the last pages of his ledger all the dealers in debt to him with the amount of each person's debt. This document must have been a powerful bargaining tool when a fisherman came to the company office during the winter to ask for new advances for the following season. Opening the general ledger must have been a mournful ritual for clients, especially as most of them could neither read nor write.

The Fruing company kept a list of good and bad debts among its dealers.4 This list reveals how a company assessed its dealers, and shows how debt, good or bad, formed a standard for judging a company's business in general and the fisherman's solvency in particular. In a generalized credit system the priority was not to make a quick profit, but to have as many good debts as possible. Whether a debt was good or bad depended on the producer's ability to repay it, but as soon as a fisherman became a good producer, with everything this implied in terms of training and mobilizing his work force, his ability to repay was eclipsed by his ability to go into debt. We shall see this later with Hyman's dealers.

In a credit system debt was a normal, almost natural phenomenon. Most dealer-producers and others had overdue accounts with their creditor, but we must distinguish between a small bill and a debt that lasts a lifetime. Debt became a form of control only when it affected dealers who had long-standing relations with a company. However, when a whole society lived on credit, individuals felt less personally responsible, psychologically, for being in debt. The fishery officer commented in 1872 about the situation of Gaspé fishermen:

> ... the majority are so used to being in debt that it becomes almost natural for them and they don't try to throw off their burden. They don't even believe it's possible to live any other way; their fathers lived like this and they've kept the habit like a tradition.[5] (translation)

This common characteristic probably helped foster a certain egalitarian ideology in Gaspé fishermen, discussed in chapter three.

Before turning to the mechanisms of indebtedness, we will first set down the criteria we have used to check samples of fishermen-dealers' accounts: they form the basis of our debt measurement.

A Sampling of Fishermen-Dealers

The best documented period in the archives of William Hyman and Sons is the second half of the 19th century, from 1854 to 1900. The ledgers we were able to consult refer mostly to the establishment at Grande-Grave and its dealers. We have taken ten consecutive years between 1854 and 1863 as a representative sample. This was the only long-term period where we could check the records for all dealers(Table 13). After this period certain ledgers are missing, and we lose the thread of the dealers' history. Also, after 1864 there were more dealers; several ledgers were used for the same year, and some of them are missing from our collection. Another reason for choosing this period was that from the 1861 census of Gaspé county we can identify and locate most of William Hyman's dealers.[6] Census data gives us the age, marital status, occupation, family situation, real estate situation, equipment and production activities of the fishermen. We also have a complete file of land transactions carried out in the Forillon area between 1842 and 1900,[7] but this data was too complex to use, given the difficulties in locating the occupants who moved quite often. A detailed analysis of these land transactions would be useful to see how land passed from owner to owner, or from father to son, and how the ever-present dependence on merchants would interfere with or prevent an inheritance.[8]

Three criteria were used as a basis for the sample: the dealer had to be a cod producer (finished product or not), he had to be a resident of the area, and he had to be a long-standing dealer of the Hyman company. Only those who had an account for all ten consecutive years were

Table 13. William Hyman and Sons, producers and production, 1854-63 (WH, hired at William Hyman's beach; PB, hired at a planter's beach; SCH, hired on board a schooner; Tot.,total hired workers)

Year	Residents	No. workers				Quintals delivered[a]	Quintals exported
		WH	PB	SCH	Tot.		
1854	103	9	1	7	17	2498	1486
1855	109	5	1	0	6	2432	2348
1856	112	18	0	4	22	3179	3350
1857	91	22	0	2	24	2418	2993
1858	131	19	11	5	35	3881	2995
1859	141	34	18	4	56	4278	6148
1860	162	21	20	3	44	5450	5796
1861	149	22	17	0	39	4273	4061
1862	164	27	8	1	36	8388	6977
1863	166	27	33	0	60	6659	7913

[a]Quintals delivered are those registered in the accounts of Hyman's dealers, whereas quintals exported are those registered the same year at the port of Gaspé. In 1856, 1857, 1859, 1860 and 1863, exports were higher than deliveries probably because production by hired help was not recorded in their accounts as most of them were salaried employees, part of the exports came from the previous year's deliveries, or Hyman may have exported under his own name some quintals belonging to another merchant with whom he had a previous agreement. In 1854, 1855, 1858, 1861 and 1862, deliveries were higher than exports probably because part of the quintals delivered were stored for the winter (winter fish) to finish drying in spring, part of them may have been damaged in transit to Gaspé, or part of them may have been exported by another merchant.

chosen, amounting to twenty-five dealers or 24 percent of all 1854 dealers (Table 14). Comparing the age-group of the 1854 sample with that of the dealers in 1860 (when the census for that year gave the age of most dealers) ensured that our sample was representative (Table 15). In both cases 85 percent of dealers were between 21 and 50, with the largest group (44%) between 31 and 40.

Grouping dealers according to their age is useful in assessing an individual's performance in a credit system, when we want to analyze conditions of social reproduction. If we assume that the merchant system perpetuated the same relations of production throughout the 19th century, then we can see how a fisherman evolved in the system from the beginning to the end of his relations with a company. Ideally, of course, we should follow the entire working life of several fishermen through their accounts. Even though Hyman's files are not complete, we can still trace the fishermen's development if we assume that the performance of a twenty-one-year-old individual corresponds to a typical performance of fishermen that age, taking into account his marital status and family situation. By examining how individuals of different ages evolved through a certain time period, we can predict how a dealer at twenty-one will perform at forty, based on the performance of other

Table 14.   List of Hyman company dealers in the 1854-63 sample.

Name	Age (1854)	Township (1861)	Locality (1861)
Aubin Fortier	22	Cap-des-Rosiers	Cap-des-Rosiers
Andrew Kassovy	24	Cap-des-Rosiers	Cap-des-Rosiers
Peter Lemesurier	25	Cap-des-Rosiers	Grande-Grave
François-Xavier Riffou	28	Cap-des-Rosiers	Cap-des-Rosiers
James Smith, Jr.	29	Cap-des-Rosiers	Cap-des-Rosiers
James Thivierge	28	Cap-des-Rosiers	Cap-des-Rosiers
John Bourgaize	35	Cap-des-Rosiers	Shiphead
John Handy	33	Gaspé north	Cap-aux-Os
John Jacques	31	Cap-des-Rosiers	Grande-Grave
Peter Kassovy	35	Cap-des-Rosiers	Anse-St-Georges
John Morris	32	Douglas	Douglastown
Michael Morris	35	Douglas	Douglastown
Thomas Morris	35	Douglas	Douglastown
Mark Packwood	31	Cap-des Rosiers	Cap-des-Rosiers
Peter Whalen	32	Cap-des-Rosiers	Cap-des-Rosiers
Philip Perrée, Jr.	38	Cap-des-Rosiers	Cap-des-Rosiers
Nicholas Price	41	Cap-des-Rosiers	Petit-Gaspé
Célestain Jacques	41	Cap-des-Rosiers	Anse-aux-Sauvages
Hilary Lenfesty	43	Cap-des-Rosiers	Cap-aux-Os
Frederick Price	41	Cap-des-Rosiers	Petit-Gaspé
Edward Price, Sr.	46	Cap-des-Rosiers	Petit-Gaspé
Jacques Eve	57	Cap-des-Rosiers	Cap-des-Rosiers
John Riffou	56	Cap-des-Rosiers	Cap-des-Rosiers
Peter Bourgaize	61	Cap-des-Rosiers	Shiphead
John Packwood	66	Cap-des-Rosiers	Cap-des-Rosiers

dealers the same age. As fishermen remained in debt from generation to generation, this exercise can reveal certain mechanisms of social reproduction. We should also take into consideration elements of the family domestic cycle. Although our approach does not include these elements, it can be a basis for their study.

Table 15. Age of William Hyman's dealers in 1854 (from sample of 25 out of 103 fishermen) and 1861 (from sample of 100 out of 162 fishermen-dealers taken from Gaspé County 1861 census).

| | 1854 | | 1861 | |
Age	%	Cumulative %	%	Cumulative %
21-25	12	12	9	9
26-30	12	24	16	25
31-35	36	60	21	46
36-40	8	68	23	69
41-45	12	80	10	79
46-50	4	84	6	85
51-55	0	84	3	88
56-60	8	92	4	92
61-65	4	96	4	96
66-70	4	100	2	98
71-75	0	100	2	100
Total	100%		100%	

In terms of consumption, for instance, we can expect a fisherman's performance to follow needs related to his family's growth. When a fisherman married, his family's consumption would naturally increase gradually with the birth and upbringing of children, reach its height when they became of working age and diminish as they left the family. This consumption cycle is predictable. In terms of production the family situation is important, especially if a fisherman had several sons who could help increase production when they reached working age. Again production peaks for at least five years before each one presumably leaves the family at age 21.[9] Of course one person's production level may have no direct relationship with his family situation, depending on his position in the production hierarchy. For instance, in our sample we find a young dealer with a large production and another important dealer who was a bachelor. We shall see later to what extent we can verify the cycle of family performance and its evolution in our sample.

Debt Factors

Before examining individual variations of indebtedness, we should first look at general trends in our sample. Nearly everyone was in debt, but there were many individual variations. As several companies operated in the Gaspé, fishermen could divide their production between two of them. Not all of Hyman's dealers dealt exclusively with him; sometimes part or most of their production went to another merchant. In a credit system, with most companies being managed similarly, a merchant's choice at the local level was influenced by companies' general practices in the area. In the last analysis we must try and see how the workings of a commercial system of several merchant companies affected the fishermen as a group, socially and economically. The companies' social impact can be judged only by bringing together all the individual experiences, and noting certain variables.

The following observations are based on an analysis of Figures 22 and 23 and Table 16. Figure 22 shows a ten-year period of growth in the Hyman company's business, already seen by the growth in exports in the same period (Fig. 3). Only twice in these ten years (1858 and 1863) did the fishermen's credits exceed their debits; in those two years their production was higher than the advances they had received, which automatically helped to lower their debt the following year. Generally, however, production was always a little lower than advances, so they

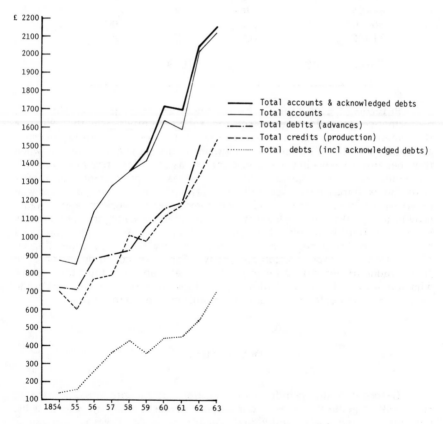

22. General trend of the transactions of twenty-five producers, 1854-63.

Table 16.   Transactions of a sample of William Hyman's dealers, 1854-63.

Year	Accounts (A) (£)	Debts (D) (£)	%D/A	Advances (Ad) (£)	Production advances (PAd) (£)	%PAd/A
1854	866	142	16	720	216	30
1855	854	163	19	709	183	26
1856	1137	255	22	879	375	43
1857	1281	363	28	912	358	39
1858	1360	427	31	933	410	44
1859	1420	355	25	1059	304	29
1860	1540	444	29	1163	471	41
1861	1595	453	28	1187	324	27
1862	2020	544	27	1507	497	33
1863	2116	698	33	1437	440	31

aWhen A is less than D+Ad, the merchant did not add a known debt of some fishermen to their annual account, but here we have added it to D. When A is greater than D+Ad, the total credit (and not D+Ad) is equal to A. In that case some fishermen recorded a slight surplus that year.

were permanently in debt. Not only did debt increase as sales rose, it also grew in proportion. Table 16 shows that in ten years the relative size of the debt doubled: in 1854 it was 16 percent of their account, in 1863 it was 33 percent, and it never returned to the level of the first years. This growth was cumulative as well: a new debt every year (the difference between debit and credit) was always added to the one not paid the year before. The company grew, dealers produced more and more, but their debt got steadily larger instead of smaller.

This is what the fishery officer noticed in 1868 when he was rejoicing a bit too soon at seeing the situation finally change. At that time, after several poor seasons, the merchants had considerably reduced their advances to fishermen, and to keep them from starving, the government had distributed grain seed to encourage agricultural development. Officer Têtu considered these two facts the beginning of a new direction for Gaspé fishermen -- they would finally understand that they had to take up agriculture to offset the disadvantages of fishing. He hoped that the disappearance of the credit system would be to their benefit, that they would no longer always have to be in debt:

With no more credit, from now on our fishermen will have to pay for their expenses with their earnings. They won't go into debt any more; they'll cultivate more, maybe fish a bit less; in short they'll live better than in the past and every year be able to pay something on the debts they ran up in the good years. Because it was in the good seasons that debts accumulated. This may seem odd when you don't know why. Take the case of a fisherman who earned $100 during the season. Of this he had to pay, say, $40 on his old debt, since there was always an old debt in one way or another, with few exceptions. Our man now had only $60 for the winter, which wasn't enough, but since he had had a good catch the previous year, since he was a good fisherman and could expect a good catch the following year, the merchant would give him an advance. Once the account was open the fisherman hardly looked at it, and his bill got higher all the time. This is why the best fishermen haven't prospered so far; this is why they find themselves without any resources in their old age after working all their lives. This is the cause of debt, and the general situation of our fishermen (except a few) who haven't cultivated any land and made fishing their only livelihood. But now everyone understands the necessity and the advantages of agriculture, for without credit you can't get flour, and only the land provides it. I am convinced that everyone is going to follow this movement and work towards this goal.10 (translation)

Four years later Napoléon Lavoie, the new fishery officer, reported the failure of agricultural development: "the inhabitants have no more taste for agriculture than their ancestors did, which helps keep them in proverty"11 (translation). When Têtu saw a smooth changeover to

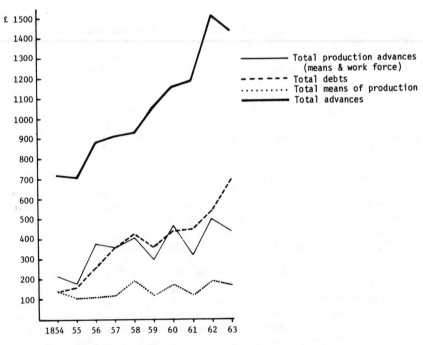

23. Details of the transactions of twenty-five producers, 1854-63.

agriculture in 1868, he underestimated the merchants' power and the system's ability to cope with variations (even large variations) in cod production. If a fisherman had any cultivated land that could feed his family, his heavy debt with a merchant could nullify his ownership rights to the land. In a time of scarcity merchants may also have favoured agricultural production, if only to keep their dealers once the scarcity was over. If fishermen weren't attracted to agriculture it wasn't only because they didn't like it. They depended on the merchants whose commercial system hinged exclusively on fishing.

Our sample and Têtu's observations show that debt increased as production increased. A good season meant increased investment in the form of larger advances, so that as Têtu says, "the best fishermen never prospered." He added that the opening of an account gave rise to reckless consumption. Forty years earlier Abbé Ferland had also denounced the compulsive consumption of luxury goods by fishermen following a good season.[12] Luxury consumption was mentioned many times (Gingras, quoted earlier, spoke of excessive consumption of tea), but we can't state categorically that it appears clearly in the 250 accounts we studied. Fishermen were said to be careless and inconsistent in their spending, and this was used later to make the fishermen responsible for perpetuating the credit system.[13] But from our data, increasing debt was mainly the result of a stimulus to production, not consumption. Larger advances bought more means of production and a larger work force.

Using correlation coefficients we measured the relationship between the debt and the total advances of the twenty-five sampled dealers during the ten-year period. The results indicate a close correlation between total debt and total advances (r: 0.91, r^2: 0.84), and also between debt and production advances (r: 0.81, r^2: 0.66):

Y	X	Y = a + b (X)	r	r^2
Advances	Debt	$Y = 482.68 + 1.48\ (X)$	0.91	0.84
Production advances	Debt	$Y = 173.30 + 0.48\ (X)$	0.81	0.66

These statistical observations tell us that for each unit increase in debt, advances increased 1.48 times. If the trend of the sample accurately reflects the trend of Hyman's dealers as a whole, then between 1854 and 1863 the company gradually raised the debt level of its fishermen, and it was capable of going higher. This is the debt level for the group as a whole: individual dealers reached a debt threshold much faster, but some of them varied considerably in their levels of advances and debt.

The capital put into circulation by the merchant in terms of advances and debts went through an annual rotation, at the end of which it grew, causing an even higher level of investment of this circulating capital. This continual rotation and redistribution affected individual dealers differently. It upset some of them continually, who for various reasons were unable to respond to its demands. A fisherman receiving a larger advance every year would suddenly find himself not getting a larger one because of a poor season. His increase had gone to someone else. What the merchant lost in one dealer's ability to produce, he gained in another. This redistribution might also be based on the merchant's preference (more or less objective) for a productive fisherman at the expense of others who were less productive. The way the merchant disposed of his capital directly influenced fishermen's activities: their advances were based on previous production. This brings us to the subject of production advances as such -- advances in means of production and money to mobilize a work force other than that of fishermen-dealers.14

Table 16 shows that on average, production advances represented 34 percent of total advances between 1854 and 1863. If production advances increased, total advances should increase measurably, as, of course, would production. Under stable technological conditions, production increased in direct proportion to an increase in the work force, which meant an increase in means of production (salt, nets, boats, etc.). Our measurement of the annual relationship between debt and production advances (r: 0.81) is significant. Figure 23 shows that in 1859 and 1861, a drop in production advances did not bring about a corresponding drop in total advances, which continued to rise. Certain reasons could be suggested for this: 1858 was one of the few years when total production was higher than total advances, which automatically lowered the debt level for 1859. Although 1859 production advances were lower, following the drop in debt, total advances went up, perhaps because producers were being encouraged to produce more. The lower production advances in 1859 were accompanied by lower production, the second in ten years. The same thing had happened in 1855. Lower production in 1859 might also be due to a poor season (Table 2 shows ecological variations). Lower production advances might also be due to a deferred investment of these advances by the company. More seasonal workers were hired in 1859 than in any other of the ten years: they increased from 19 in 1858 to 34 in 1859 (Table 13). These seasonal producers may have been fostered to the detriment of resident producers. Hyman recruited more seasonal workers in a poor season to cut his production costs.

In 1861 production advances were lower, whereas total advances stayed the same (or slightly higher), as did debt. The drop in production advances had no effect on sample dealers' total production this time as it rose slightly. This variation is difficult to explain when we refer to the factors that explained the 1859 variation. In 1859 the higher production in our sample corresponded to an increase in ·the Hyman's company's total exports (Fig. 3), whereas in 1861 production was slightly higher in our sample, but considerably fewer quintals of cod were exported. It was in 1861 that the Port of Gaspé was declared a free port, a status that lasted until 1866. Table 1 shows that exports by the four major companies in the Gaspé were considerably lower for those six years. Possibly small local merchants (and maybe also the Robin company) took away much of Hyman's business during those years, accounting for his lower total exports.

Except for yearly variations which can be problematic, we know that in these ten years there was a steady increase in debt, advances and production, which means that there was a direct relationship between potential for debt and level of production.

Merchant capital in the form of debt was in the long run good debt (productive), rather than bad debt (unproductive), in the sense that debt increased because merchants invested more in the fishermen's ability to produce. To understand this we must distinguish between the origin of debt and its growth. Debt originated because the product of one fishing season could almost never equal the sum of annual advances to the fishermen. As Têtu said, "in one way or another, with few exceptions, there was always an old debt." However, the steady growth of the initial debt did not result simply from a cumulative effect of the old debt, but much more from a stimulus to production. In a credit system, and with a short fishing season, debt ensured increased production.

Annual variations in fishermen's accounts and differences between them may be due to several factors. The family environment and family growth were certainly determining factors, but they require separate treatment. We will consider only observable evidence that can be found in the accounts themselves. We will not attempt to explain the many variations from year to year and from one individual to another, but we shall try to pinpoint the main factors when variations are particularly noticeable either in debt level, advances or production. Our approach here is more empirical than analytical: we have tried to show how interruptions in fishermen's individual production cycles fitted into the company's total production cycle during a growth period. Table 17 gives the widest variations in sixteen of the twenty-five accounts in our sample (the nine others did not show any noteworthy variations in performance). In ten of the sixteen cases the growth in debt was directly linked to growth in production effort. We see an almost classic progression in these accounts: the fisherman received higher advances for means of production (MP), they paid out salaries (Pa), gave credit notes or cash to other fishermen, their cod production (P) increased, and at the start of the following year their debt (D) increased sharply. Table 17 gives this progression in the following symbols:

$$(+ MP + Pa + P) \longrightarrow +D$$

In three cases the increased debt had to be acknowledged by a signature: this was usually registered as a bond at the Percé registry office. When a fisherman had to sign a note of hand, this didn't automatically exclude him from being a dealer, at least in the short run. In the case of one fisherman, Aubin Fortier, his debt seems to have led him to give up fishing, at least for one season, when he became a miner in 1864. Another fisherman, F.X. Riffou, continued to produce. In the last case, P. Whalen, his advances even increased -- he was probably more solvent, being the owner of a schooner. In one case, James Smith, Jr. bought a fishing establishment and worked on salary for two and half a months. The following year his debt increased and he sold some property, which lowered his debt considerably the following year. Two individuals, Aubin Fortier and John Jacques, inherited two additional debts from relatives or associates. Finally, large sums were deposited to the credit of two big producers, Peter Kassovy and Hilary Lenfesty, by

Table 17. Evolution of sample dealer transactions (1854-63).

CLIENTS	1854	1855	1856	1857	1858	1859	1860	1861	1862	1863
AUBIN FORTIER [1]			DS	MP	D+			NH	NH	NH
*ANDREW KASSOVY					P+,MP+	PA+			D+	D+
PETER LEMESURIER			PA	D+						
F.X. RIFFOU						P-	D+ NH	NH	NH	NH
JAMES SMITH JR						PA+ ET+ TS	D+ V			
JAMES THIVIERGE										
JOHN BOURGAIZE [2]							MP+ P+			
JOHN HANDY					MP	MP	D+			
JOHN JACQUES				P-	DS	PA D+				
*PETER KASSOVY [3]				MP+ PA+ P+	D+	P-	MP+ PA+ P+	D+ P-	PA+ P+	P- D+
JOHN MORRIS [4]							CR			
MICHAEL MORRIS [5]										
THOMAS MORRIS [6]										
MARK PACKWOOD										
*PETER WHALEN [7]						NH	NH	NH	NH MP+ P+ D+	MP+ P+ D+
PH PERREE JR							ET P+			
NICHOLAS PRICE [8]									MP+ P+	MP+ P+
*CELESTAIN JACQUES [9]			ET MP+ PA+ P							
*HILARY LENFESTY [10]			MP+ PA+ P+	D	CR	P-				
FREDERICK PRICE										
EDWARD PRICE SR.										
JACQUES EVE										
JOHN RIFFOU										
PETER BOURGAIZE [11]							MP+	D+	D-	
JOHN PACKWOOD					MP+ PA+ P+		MP+	PA+ PA+		

[1] Worked as a miner in 1864.
[2] Almost never in debt; in 1860 was paid cash for part of his production.
[3] No debt registered to his account of 186, but in 1860 paid interest on advances received; the Fruing Co. gave him £109.8.4 1/2 credit in 1860.
[4] Almost never in debt.
[5] Almost never in debt; in 1860 was paid cash for most of his production; mostly draft fisherman.
[6] Almost never in debt.
[7] He and his brother Matthew owned the schooner *Fancy*.
[8] Became a true dealer-producer in 1861 when he bought a large amount of flour (£12).
[9] Almost never in debt; was paid cash for most of his production; beginning in 1859 received a 5 percent discount on his advances.
[10] Hired the schooner *Sam* in 1857; in 1858 the Fruing Co. put £41 to his credit and £10 in 1860; account was never very high after that; probably went over to Fruing.
[11] Almost never in debt.

DS: Additional debt to a relative or associate.
MP: Means of production.
D: Debt.
NH: Note of Hand, i.e. a signed acknowledgement of debt; payments spread over four years.
Pa: Payments for an increase in work force.
P: Production.
ET: Payments made on a fishing establishment.
TS: Salaried work.
V: Sale of property.
CR: Money deposited to a fisherman's account by Fruing Co.; usually means the fisherman changed company.
* Major producers (planters).
+ Increase.
- Decrease.

the Fruing company, most likely indicating a change of creditor, only temporary in Kassovy's case.

A systematic analysis of individual variations in debt would require a special study that would include family and real estate evolution over a long period. Our sample, however, gives us a dealer relationship over a ten-year period. In spite of the diversity in ages, family and land situations and, no doubt, professional fishing establishments of different sizes, we can see the same progression in production growth, which means that in only a few years individual debt could reach critical proportions for most of the producers.

Continual Debt and the Merchant System

Debt as a phenomenon of economic dependence served three functions: it initiated production, it increased production, and it ensured the reproduction of all aspects of production. These functions corresponded to three stages of indebtedness: creation, growth and reproduction. Once initiated, debt ensured the loyalty of fishermen to the merchant from generation to generation, and their desire to get out of debt by producing more resulted in increased debt. Increased production always fostered the illusion that the debt could be paid, yet increased production was conditional on increased debt. This is where the strength of the merchant system came from, because it was exactly this effort of the fishermen to free themselves from debt that guaranteed its continuance. In an ideological climate that encouraged work and effort, people took it for granted that you stayed in debt only because you didn't work hard enough. Although we have been able to analyze this system on an accounting and economic basis, we certainly cannot ignore the importance of this fetishistic attitude toward work as an explanation of its survival over such a long period.

CONCLUSION

From our initial hypotheses, we proposed to look at 19th century Gaspé economic and social life as a focal point for the articulation, expansion and reproduction of merchant capital of a maritime area. Having established that Gaspé from the end of the 18th to the end of the 19th century was part of the great network of British Atlantic trade, we realized that internal dynamics of the production process of dried cod were governed by the circulation of commodities, which was the major component of merchant capital. This circulation, because of its driving strength and because of the kinds of commodities it brought into play, also brought many producers into circulation. On the question of land, we saw that by supplying producers with provisions on credit, merchant capital was able to seize control of the fishing plants by controlling the producers, forcing them to move and be replaced.[1] The control over producers did not come about in terms of strictly capitalist social relationships based on salary, which was only partially used by the merchants. We believe it was this two-way ciculation that explains the basis of the economic system in 19th century Gaspé, and bringing this process to light allowed us to understand not only how the system emerged and became consolidated, but also how it collapsed so quickly at the end of the century.

Putting merchant capital into the Gaspé was not the first experience overseas for British capitalists. Their action was partly modeled on similar previous endeavours in the Caribbean[2] and partly conditioned by the American War of Independence, which forced them to move farther north. It was also in the 19th and 20th centuries that the Hudson's Bay Company occupied the Canadian north trapping foxes.[3] Merchant capital in Gaspé also operated in many ways like similar practices in South and Central America, where absentee landlords ruled the economy and continual debt was the key variable in controlling the work force.[4]

The main factors governing the adaptation of this economic system to the area are the following:

1. The determining factor was not the exploitation of a single resource, cod, but the fact that this resource, because of its mobility and the relatively short fishing season, made any long-term economic planning difficult.

2. As in many fishing operations where çatching, transporting and processing fish are carried out in different places, dried cod production had to be based on a fairly elaborate technical division of labour.

3. Finally, the input of British merchant capital in Gaspé came about in a negative demographic context which obliged entrepreneurs to develop additional mechanisms of control over the producers -- mechanisms seen clearly in the diversity of production units. Although such diversity was also found in the development of merchant capital for agricultural exploitation elsewhere in the Americas, it never existed with the same intensity as in Gaspé, where around the same curing beach would gravitate independent fishermen, associates and salaried workers.

24. Grande-Grave harbour in 1969. (Photo by Dalton Muir)

The specific requirements of cod fishing, as well as the initial absence of workers in the area, imposed special limits on Anglo-Norman entrepreneurs and their imitators that have led us to declare, without necessarily speaking of the real relations of capitalist production, that the circulation of merchandise was always accompanied by a circulation of producers.

It was this apparent contradiction (well illustrated by the establishment of mechanisms of control over producers' mobility such as credit, debt and legal recourse) that explained the collapse of the system. From this point of view this study is interesting to any economic anthropologist studying economies in transition or the problem of underdevelopment. How, in fact, could a system of exploitation that managed to survive and expand over such a long period suddenly disappear?

We can certainly point to conjectural factors linked to a broader economic context or even to the proliferation of internal competition. Certain Gaspé entrepreneurs in fact suddenly abandoned their business because the banking institutions supporting them went bankrupt. But these bankruptcies, because of the very nature of finance capital, were not necessarily due to poor fishing seasons. They were no doubt caused by losses due to poor investments in other sectors of production. Internal competition cannot be considered a determining element either, for it was present at the beginning of the 19th century and enabled the economic system to survive and expand.[5] Then, given the anarchistic nature of capital and certain companies' privileged position in maritime trade and marketing, competition gradually reinforced their control,

25. Beach, ramp and buildings: Clarence Roberts cove, Shiphead, 1970. (Photo by Maxime St-Amour)

leading to a monopoly situation. How do we then explain the breakdown of the system so soon after solid monopolies were established?

Analyzing the evolution of the Gaspé economic system, we realize that in spite of its progression and expansion in land area and number of people,6 its capital structure was always weak in the sense that the technological basis that represented fixed capital never prospered in relation to the working capital, the growth of the work force. Around 1900 the basic technology was the same as one hundred years before. Then we realize that an increase in production did not actually correspond to an increase in productivity, and that under the guise of area expansion and a capitalist trend toward concentration, entrepreneurs could count on income that was merely stable or even decreasing.7 At the end of the 19th century, when Norwegian and American competition arrived on the scene, based on production units with a stronger capital structure, Gaspé entrepreneurs found they were producing more and more at a loss and lost their competitive edge on international markets.

The merchants departed, leaving Gaspé fishermen with but a memory of a long exploitation, prolonged by an outmoded paternalism, with the only possible alternative of a cooperative system in which they would all be equal. However, in setting up this system hoping to better their economic sistuation within an already capitalist system, they made the same mistake as the entrepreneurs in staking everything on "controlling" producers and keeping the same technological base.

APPENDICES

Appendix A. Merchants of Gaspé Bay and the Forillon Peninsula in 1862.

Locality	Merchants	Type of business
Pointe-St-Pierre	J. & E. Collas	dried cod
Pointe-St-Pierre	John Fauvel	dried cod
Douglastown	Charles Veit	dried cod
Douglastown	William Lindsay	dried cod
Gaspé Basin	John Le Boutillier	dried cod
Gaspé Basin	Fruing & Co.	dried cod
Gaspé Basin	Nicolas Dumaresq	dried cod
Gaspé Basin	Lowndes & Bros	dried cod
Gaspé Basin	John Slous	dry goods
Gaspé Basin	Georges Dumaresq	dried cod
Gaspé Basin	Horatio Dolbel	grocery
Gaspé Basin	John McKay	dry goods, grocery
Gaspé Basin	Ed. Jones	dry goods, grocery
Gaspé Basin	Jos. Eden	grocery, etc.
Grande-Grave	Fruing & Co.	dried cod
Grande-Grave	Wm. Hyman	dried cod
Grande-Grave	Nicolas Dumaresq	dried cod
Anse-St-Georges	Ed. Perry	dried cod
Anse-au-Griffon	Fruing & Co.	dried cod
Anse-au-Griffon	John Le Boutillier	dried cod
Rivière-au-Renard	L.A. Blouin & Co.	dried cod
Rivière-au-Renard	James De Ste-Croix	dried cod
Rivière-au-Renard	J.A. Le Couteur	dried cod
Rivière-au-Renard	G. Dumaresq	dried cod
Petite-Rivière-au-Renard	Narcisse Bernier	dried cod

Appendix B. Hyman company and Fruing company land transactions in Forillon and the north coast of Gaspé.

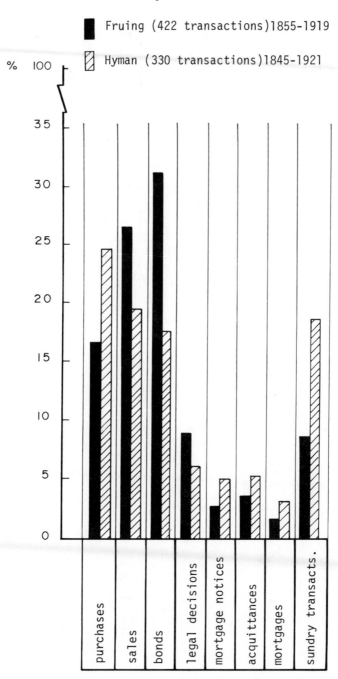

Appendix C. William Hyman's annual activities from his 1864–65 correspondence.

Months (columns): January, February, March, April, May, June, July, August, September, October, November, December

COD CARGOES

- Returns on cargoes of previous summer (January–February)
- Returns on spring shipwrecks (August)
- Returns on spring cargoes (October–November)
- Arrangements with Jersey broker (February–March)
- Chartering ships, winter fish (March)
- Chartering ships, summer fish (May)
- Chartering ships, fall fish (August)
- Insuring cargoes (March)
- Winter fish, arrival & departure of ships (April–May)
- Summer & fall fish, arrival & departure of ships (July–October)
  - 1st arriv. (July), 2nd arriv. (August), 3rd arriv. (September), 4th arriv. (November)
  - 1st dep. (July), 2nd dep. (October), 3rd dep. (November), 4th dep. (December)

SUPPLIES: MERCHANDISE & RAW MATERIALS

- Orders from Europe (January)
- Salt orders (April)
- Orders from Quebec (April–May)
- Arrival of merchandise from Quebec (May–June)
- Arrival of merchandise from Europe (June–July)
- Arrival of salt (June–July)
- Arrival of salt (September)
- Arrival of salt (November)

FISHING SEASON: PREPARATIONS & ONGOING ACTIVITIES

- Arrangements with agents & clerks (February)
- Repairs to gear & rigging (March–April)
- Recruiting hired workers & advances for trip (April)
- Advances on winter fish (April)
- Advances on summer fish (May)
- Arrival of Jersey clerk (May)
- Arrival of hired workers (June)
- Summer fishing (July–August)
- Anticosti fishing (July–August)
- Departure of hired workers (September–October)
- Fall fishing (September–October)
- Weighing (September)
- Departure of clerk (December)

Appendix D. William Hyman's establishments in 1865.

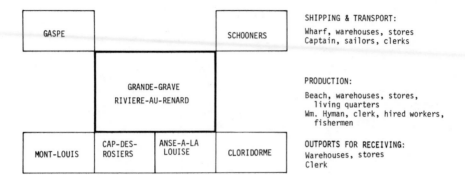

				SHIPPING & TRANSPORT:
GASPE			SCHOONERS	Wharf, warehouses, stores Captain, sailors, clerks

PRODUCTION:

Beach, warehouses, stores,
    living quarters
Wm. Hyman, clerk, hired workers,
    fishermen

OUTPORTS FOR RECEIVING:
Warehouses, stores
Clerk

Appendix E. William Hyman and Sons' circulation and types of capital ca. 1865.

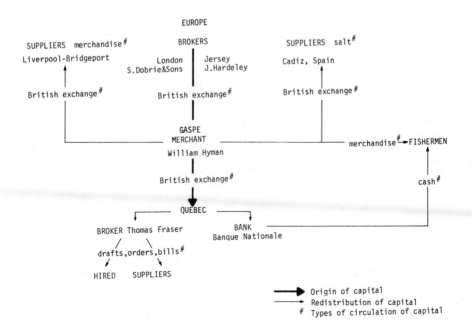

Appendix F.   Origin and distribution of William Hyman's cod cargoes (1865).

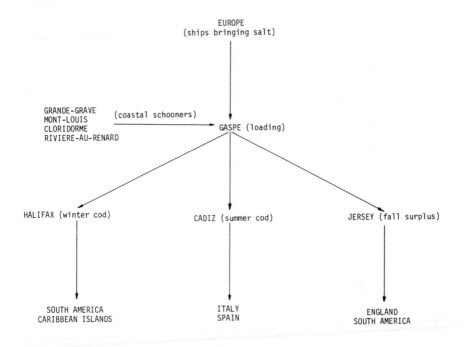

Appendix G.   Cod cargoes shipped by William Hyman in 1864 and 1865.

Date	Ship	Quintals	Destination	Buyer
1864				
21/6	Boadina	107.0	Barbades	Cavan
15/6	Belus	1030.5	Naples (via Cadix)	Mainguy & Robin
23/9	Richard	1995.0	Cadix	Shaw
29/10	Azalia	1558.0	Civitavecchia	Low & Brothers
7/10	Queen of Isles	1734.0	Cadix	Shaw
25/11	Belus	2010.0	Naples (via	Low & Brothers
	Total	8434.5	Civitavecchia)	
1865				
16/10	Volunteer	1548.0	Bari (via Cadix)	Matthewson
17/11	Why Not	2568.0	Ancona (via Cadix)	Le Mesurier
18/11	Priscilla	2235.0	Cadix	Shaw
29/11	Chance	700.0	Naples (via Cadix)	
	Total	7051.0		

Appendix H.   A large company fishing establishment.

Production areas	Living areas	Commercial areas	Agricultural areas
beach	grande maison	store	farm (bldgs)
boats (barges	cookrooms	office	fields
and flats)	well	warehouses	pastures
stage head			woods
and splitting			
cabin			
stage			
trough			
saline			
warehouses			
net-drying racks			
flakes			
cooperage			
forge			

Appendix I. Merchant capital in Gaspé: production and circulation.

The Hyman company's ledgers and business correspondence are a record of transactions between Hyman and his fishermen-dealers, on both consumption and production levels. The data are accurate: day-to-day relationships can be seen over a long period by looking at many individual accounts. This documentation is invaluable, because it shows how social relations perpetuated themselves over a period of five generations, from 1770 to around 1920, and how they influenced production. By studying the performance of the fishermen as it evolved, their socio-economic conditions can be determined precisely, and the phenomenon of social differentiation that arose from the dried cod production process can be brought to light. In providing more accurate data about the merchant system in the Gaspé, we hope to fill an important gap and forestall any future attempt to hastily simplify the real world of 19th century Gaspé.

In this study, the steps involved in the dried cod production process had to be made clear because of the specialized nature of Gaspé production. The settlement and development of the Gaspé area can be seen clearly only by examining the implications of the particular type of system used in the 19th century to develop the fishing industry. Far from being simple colonists looking for a patch of land to settle, the first inhabitants, beginning in 1760, were entrepreneurs whose efforts were focused on developing cod fishing and producing dried cod.[1] The land was first settled for commercial purposes at a time when Mediterranean and Caribbean markets needed to be supplied with dried cod, notably Gaspé cod, to which they had become accustomed because of French development of the market. Settlement and development were left entirely to merchants' initiative and were only slightly affected by government intervention.

As merchants controlled the exploitation of maritime resources in the Gaspé area, the way these resources were developed was an important factor in determining the history and population of the area. Seen from a broader economic perspective, Gaspé merchant enterprise was only one of the components of merchant capitalism that dominated the entire network of Atlantic fisheries in the 18th and 19th century. If we look at the characteristics of merchant capital, we can see how and on what basis it operated in the Gaspé context.

Two concepts are important here: the production process and the circulation process. Before these concepts and their relevance to the Gaspé situation are explained, we would like to link them with two major phenomena that historiography has shown us, to enable the reader to judge their relevance. In assessing the fishermen's dependence on the merchant monopoly, contemporary observers pointed out two things: the fact that all food supplies for the area came from outside, and the fishermen's continual state of debt.[2] As fishermen specialized in one type of production, they had to turn to merchants for provisions and means of production. The credit system made this possible, but by its very definition it put them into debt, and they remained in debt once their production was finished. Circulation and production were two sides of a single coin: without supplies and provisions (brought in from outside) there could be no production. An external process thus determined an internal one from the very beginning. We are now going to return to more theoretical concepts and see more closely how concepts of production and circulation processes can help us understand 19th century production of dried cod.

The concepts should first be defined. According to Marxian analysts, the production process defines the work process or processes as determined by the relations of production.[3] This is what Rey, following Marx, identifies as the immediate production process in a restricted sense, which is different from the process of social production and what Marx calls "the real process of production, that is, the immediate circulation process and the distribution process together."

> This difference between the isolated act of production and pro-
> duction in its social significance comes from the fact that the
> latter is not only production but reproduction; besides production in
> the limited sense it also includes circulation and in particular that
> part of it which is worker consumption.[4] (translation)

The production process for dried cod in the Gaspé was an immediate production process. The men and women employed in the different work processes (fishing and fish processing) were employed under specific conditions called here production relations, which were dictated by the requirements of merchant capital, that is by the necessitites of circulation of commodities.

According to Rey, Marx saw distribution as the "exchange of commodities between capitalists and only between capitalists." He makes it clear that this is "an exchange between the capitalist who supplies consumer goods to the worker and the capitalist who uses his work force. The fact that the worker consumes the product is merely incidental to the circulation process: it adds no value to the product consumed" because the labour of the worker is itself a commodity. Circulation plays a double role in capitalist production: "in every aspect it reproduces technical and social aspects of production simultaneously."[5]

These definitions can be useful to us. According to Marx's analysis of capitalism, production covers several processes apparently isolated from each other. Here we make dried cod, there we make nets, clothes and furniture. These products are then distributed and become commodities that middlemen buy from producers to sell to consumers. Capitalists assume the responsibility of instigating production and others take on the job of selling it. Production and circulation are thus separate but equal and necessary to each other; if the producer wants to produce more, the previous product has to be sold. But Marx argues that production processes are interrelated by the very fact of the circulation of commodities and this constitutes the real process of production in its effects on society. Its social effects are seen in the work force as consumers. In his theory of work-value[6], Max has shown that workers, who are the actual producers in capitalist factories, are not paid according to the real value of the product but according to standards, based on work time, that allow the worker to reproduce himself physically. The difference between the selling price of a product and its production cost is the capitalist's profit. The worker consumes supplies, clothes, etc., in order to provide future work. It is in this sense that Marx sees the work force as a commodity, because it is literally bought and sold in exchange for other consumer products.7 This is why he sees circulation as "an exchange between the capitalist who supplies consumer goods to the worker and the capitalist who uses the work force." In the game of circulation workers employed under the capitalist system have their place: as consumers they guarantee "the reproduction of all technical and social relations of production simultaneously."

The entire production process in Gaspé was conditioned from beginning to end by the circulation process: at the start, supplying means of production (salt, tackle, gear, rigging), supplies (flour, etc.) and other means of subsistence, and at the end, disposal of the product, dried cod, using the same circulation infrastructure (ocean schooners) that brought supplies. The production process was here only one aspect of the circulation of all merchandise exchanged by capitalists. Fishermen consumed supplies and means of production in order to produce dried cod, which when sold on the market raised capital to supply them so that production could begin again. The work force of the fishermen brought the circulation system full circle, at which point merchant capital invested in it realized a profit. A formal model follows which shows where fishermen-producers fit into the cycle of merchant capital.

Merchant capital that found its way to the Gaspé, as we have seen with the Hyman company, was actually financial capital -- a surplus of industrial capital in England. This surplus was used to broaden the circulation of commodities produced by industrial capital and was supposed to increase the capital. For the initial value of the capital to complete its growth cycle, which we may term $A - M - A'$, capital that bought commodities in England had to find fertile ground for growth in the Gaspé. With the $A - M - A'$ formula, £100 sterling to buy commodities in England had to become £110 sterling once the commodities arrived in the Gaspé.8 The trouble in the Gaspé was that the £100 did not exist in cash. In return for the £100 he invested, the capitalist received a certain amount of dried cod, and only when the cod was sold did his capital A become A'. To complete the cycle $A - M - A'$, the first phase $A - M$ is easily understandable, whereas the second phase $M - A'$ is not so simple. To complete the sale of the first commodity, another commodity M" had to be produced (dried cod), and only when this was sold could the initial capital A become increased capital A'. It was in the $A - M' - M" - A'$ process that the concepts of production process and circulation process become meaningful.

Commodities (including essential means of production like salt and fishing gear) had to be put into the system to allow the completion of the production process, essential for the capital investment to grow. The work force had to be reliable and also reproduce. Fishermen in continual debt guaranteed that the system went on reproducing, and this debt was rooted in the circulation process -- provision of commodities and outflow of product, these two phases operating under the credit system. In light of the broader perspective of the merchant capital cycle, 19th century Gaspé is doubly interesting in that the same capitalists were at the same time responsible for distributing commodities and initiating its production, whereas under industrial capitalism then developing in England, merchants distributed only what manufacturers produced. In the colonial period in America it was the merchants who initiated production. Subject to the requirements of commercial capital, production processes thus initiated are of particular interest in that they were not based on wage earning as a dominant production relation. This is why it is important to look closely at the production process for dried cod in 19th century Gaspé, because social relationships stemming from the control of production by merchant capital took different paths from those of industrial capitalism, and our perception of this difference can help to better understand the special characteristics of the maritime population of the Gulf of St. Lawrence.

It is from this overall theoretical perspective that we looked at the way the production process for dried cod developed in the case of William Hyman and Sons and its fishermen-dealers.

ENDNOTES

Introduction

1   On merchants' monopolies and fishermen dependency see Antoine Bernard, La Gaspésie au soleil (Montreal: C.S.V., 1925), p. 182, on remarks by Msgr. Plessis in 1811; Dr. Anthony Von Iffland, "Aperçu d'un voyage dans le district de Gaspé pendant les mois de mai, juin, juillet et une partie d'août 1821...." Revue d'histoire de la Gaspésie, Vol. 7, No. 1 (Jan.-Mar. 1969), p. 32; J.-B.-A. Ferland, "Journal d'un voyage sur les côtes de la Gaspésie," les soirées canadiennes, Quebec, 1861, pp. 410-11; Canada. Annual Report of the Gulf of St. Lawrence Fisheries Officer, Rapport de Pierre Fortin, 1859, pp. 69-70 and 1864, p. 37; Rapport de Napoléon Lavoie, 1874, annexe 3, p. 4. The annual reports refer to the following sources: 1854-67, Appendices des journaux de l'assemblée législative de la Province du Canada. Rapports de Pierre Fortin (hereafter cited as Rapports Fortin); 1868, Département de la marine et des pêcheries, Document de la session n° 12. Rapports de Théophile Têtu (hereafter cited as Rapport Têtu); 1868-79, Département de la marine et des pêcheries, Documents de la session. Rapports de Napoléon Lavoie (hereafter cited as Rapports Lavoie); 1880-1914, Département de la marine et des pêcheries, Documents de la session. Rapports de William Wakeham (hereafter cited as Rapports Wakeham).

2   On the inhabitants of Bonaventure County, see Joseph Sansfaçon's article in the Gazette des campagnes, Oct. 15, 1866, p. 190: "However, it is regrettable every year to see many, or, to tell the whole truth, most of the young men go off fishing and not come back till the autumn. As a patriot I feel sick seeing that bunch of strong, vigorous young men go away, far away, often to lose their health and virtue; whereas if they stayed under the paternal roof, they would contribute to the general well-being, and more easily preserve their health and their virtuous ways. We may add that for some years now fishing is so unproductive that most of them who go in for it come back in debt. It is God's will, so that we may understand where we should seek true wealth. It was said to man: cultivate the earth, that is the human family's vocation (my underlining). We need more hard-working Christian farmers: society will be more peaceful and happy, the better to fulfill its destiny." (translation)

3   See André Lepage, "Histoire de la population et du peuplement de la péninsule de Forillon," Manuscript on file, National Historic Parks and Sites Branch, Parks Canada, 1978, pp. 73-78.

4   In a 1926 biography of William Hyman we read, "He was generously disposed towards the poor and needy and gave assistance to many families in their want. He advanced provisions to the poor on the Gaspé coast in the winter especially when they could get none anywhere else, and as the people in their poverty were unable to repay him, he incurred great losses through his generosity." (my underlining); The Jew in Canada..., Arthur Daniel Hart, comp.,

(Montreal: Jewish Publications, 1926); see also Francis M. Gibaut, "Memories of a Gaspesian", Revue d'histoire de la Gaspésie, Vol. 1, No. 1 (Jan.-Mar. 1963), p. 31.

5   The debate came up again recently when a group of Paspébiac citizens decided to restore the Paspébiac fishing bank in Chaleur Bay, the site of the most powerful Jersey company in the 18th and 19th centuries, Charles Robin and Company; see Bernard Nadeau and Pierre Provost, "Renovation of Historical Buildings", Spec (Gaspé), Vol. 3, No. 7 (Oct. 3, 1977), and the reply of a former agent of the Robin company to their statements on the exploitation and domination of the company; Arthur G. Legros, "Refutation of an Old Fantasy," Spec (Gaspé), Vol. 3, No. 8 (24 Oct. 1977).

6   Harold A. Innis, The Cod Fisheries; the History of an International Economy (Toronto, University of Toronto Press, 1978), p. 494.

7   Fernand Ouellet, Histoire économique et sociale du Québec, 1760-1850; Structures et conjoncture (Montreal: Fides, 1966), p. 304.

8   Jean Hamelin and Yves Roby, Histoire économique du Québec, 1851-1896 (Montreal: Fides, 1971), Pt. 3, Ch. 4, "Le monde des pêcheries."

I   William Hyman and Sons

1   In the 1861 census, Hyman's business is identified as "William Hyman and Co." This was the only time the name "company" was used in the 19th century. Elsewhere it is William Hyman "trader" or "merchant." From 1883 on, the company is called "William Hyman and Sons," and beginning in 1925, "William Hyman and Sons Ltd." In the text "company" is used to designate his enterprise because his status was that of an import and export company, as was the Fruing company, which was clearly designated as such.

2   Roch Samson, "Gaspé, 1760-1830: l'action du capital marchand chez les pêcheurs," Anthropologie et Sociétés, Vol. 5, No. 1 (Spring 1981), hereafter cited "Gaspé."

3   Dr. Anthony Von Iffland, op. cit.

4   David Lee, "La Gaspésie, 1760-1867," Lieux historiques canadiens: cahiers d'archéologie et d'histoire, No. 23 (1980), pp. 149-50.

5   Ibid., p. 150.

6   Ibid.

7   Percé. Bureau d'enregistrement (hereafter cited as PBE), Registre B, Vol. 2, p. 567, No. 1159, 1855.

8   David Lee, op. cit., p. 155.

9   See chapter two, section on assessment of the work force.

10   E.-C. Woodley, "The Hymans of Gaspé", Revue d'histoire de la Gaspésie, Vol. 11, No. 2 (April-June 1973), pp. 74-78.

11   Canada. Parks Canada (hereafter cited as PC), private archives of David Hyman (hereafter cited as ADH), Letterbooks, 1864-66, letter to Abraham Joseph, Feb. 27, 1866, and first letter in endnote 12 following. Joseph was president of the National Bank in 1864, letter to E.-B. Harris, July 12, 1864.

12   Ibid, Letterbooks, 1864-66, letters to Thomas Fraser, Quebec broker, July 6, 1864, and to Jersey broker John Hardeley, Apr. 14, 1865.

112

13 PBE, Registre B, Vol. 1, No. 292, p. 252, 1845.

14 PC, ADH, Letterbooks, 1864-66, letter to E. Martel, a New Carlisle lawyer, May 2, 1865. Many records must have been destroyed in the fire.

15 Thérèse Savoie, "Historique des établissements de pêche et compagnies de Grande-Grave," Manuscript on file, Recherches historiques, Parks Canada, Quebec (1978).

16 Ibid., p. 35.

17 PC, ADH, Letterbooks, 1882-1884, Jan. 1883, pp. 69-77.

18 Ibid., letter to M. Tremblay, New Carlisle lawyer, Dec. 11, 1882.

19 PBE, Registre B, Vol. 28, p. 605, No. 3853, June 24, 1919.

20 Ibid., Vol. 99, Registration No. 47982, Aug. 1, 1967.

21 At an outpost or station advances in merchandise were made to clients in exchange for a promise to deliver fish. This did not prevent other transactions from going on there as well.

22 PBE, Registre B, Vol. 5, p. 404, No. 307, Apr. 4, 1865, agreement between William Hyman and John De Ste-Croix of Rivière-au-Renard.

23 PC, ADH, Letterbooks, 1864-66, letter to Horatio Dolbel, his agent at Mont-Louis, Sept. 21, 1864.

24 Ibid., letter to John Hardeley, his broker in Jersey, May 30, 1865.

25 See chapter two, section on types of fishing.

26 PC, ADH, Letterbooks, 1864-66, letter to Thomas Fraser, Apr. 12, 1864, and to W. Drum, Sept. 27, 1864.

27 Ibid., letter to John Hardeley, July 19, 1864.

28 Ibid., letter to Thomas Fraser, May 20, 1864.

29 Ibid., letters to A. Joseph, Feb. 4, 1864, and to E.-B. Harris, July 12, 1864.

30 Jean Hamelin and Yves Roby, op. cit., p. 234.

31 Dictionary of Canadian Biography (Toronto: University of Toronto Press, 1982), Vol. II, s.v. "William Hyman."

32 PC, ADH, Letterbooks, 1864-66, letter to Moses Levy & Co. of London, May 31, 1865; letters to Aaron and Jane Loryea, May 14, 1865.

33 Ibid.

34 Ibid., Letterbooks, 1877-79, letter to Clark & Rowe of London, Dec. 3, 1877.

35 PC, ADH, Letterbooks, 1864-66, letter to H. Dolbel, Apr. 3, 1865.

36 PC, ADH, Correspondence from Jersey Brokers, Edward De La Perrelle to William Hyman, Sept. 14, 1869.

37 Ibid., Letterbooks, 1864-66, letter to John Hardeley, Jan. 17, 1865.

38 Ibid., letters to I.G.A. Creighton of Halifax, Feb. 9, 1864 and Mar. 23, 1864.

39 Ibid., letter to John Hardeley, Feb. 13, 1866.

40 Ibid., letter to John De Ste-Croix, Apr. 29, 1864.

41 The Fruing Company was actually blackmailing Hyman's fishermen: "To crown all Capt. Mann who is gone to Carleton for a load of potatoes is not back yet and my neighbour [Fruing] says to my dealers if you take salt from me I will let you have potatoes." Ibid., letter to Horatio Dolbel, his agent at Mont-Louis, May 16, 1866.

42   PC, ADH, Correspondence from Jersey Brokers, John Hardeley to Samuel Dobrie & Sons of London, Dec. 3, 1868.
43   Ibid., Edward De La Perrelle to William Hyman, July 6, 1869.
44   PBE, Registre B, Vol. 28, p. 163, No. 3506, Oct. 17, 1918 (Cloridorme establishment bought for $1500); ibid., p. 231, No. 3572, July 8, 1925 (Grande-Grave establishment bought for $2500).

II Production of Dried Cod: Technical Aspects and Work Force

1   For further details see Charles de La Morandière, Histoire de la pêche française de la morue dans l'Amérique septentrionale (Paris: Maisonneuve and Larose, 1962-66), 3 vols.
2   Schooners and "clubs" of sailor-fishermen doing fishing and coastal transport for the Hyman company from 1856 to 1859: 1856 Agnès, Canopus; 1857 Native, Agnès; 1858 Agnès, St-Ignace; 1859 Agnès, St-Ignace. PC, William Hyman and Sons archives (hereafter cited as WHS), Ledgers, 1856-59. In two letters addressed to Captain Coulombe of Cloridorme, Hyman asks him if he wants to go and fish at Anticosti Island. He also says that Douglastown fishermen have been going to Bell Bay, Anticosti, for three years. PC, ADH, Letterbooks, 1864-66, letters of Mar. 29 and Apr. 29, 1864. In another letter to Captain Coulombe on Feb. 17, 1865, Hyman says that fishing was good at Anticosti in 1864 in spite of a poor season at Gaspé. Schooner crews consisted of six or seven men.
3   A measure of 238 pounds of salted or fresh cod.
4   PC, ADH, Letterbooks, 1864-66, letter to I.-E. Collas of Pointe Saint-Pierre, June 13, 1865: quantities of bait but no cod. Ibid., letter to John Hardeley of Jersey, June 6, 1866: good quantity of capelin and herring but no cod. Rapports Fortin, 1858, p. 34: abundant cod, no bait.
5   Rapports Fortin, 1859, p. 66.
6   PC, ADH, Letterbooks, 1864-66, letter to Têtu & Garneau of Quebec City, Aug. 8, 1865.
7   Ibid., letter to Edward De La Perrelle, merchant of Cape Cove, Aug. 12, 1865.
8   Ibid., Letterbooks, 1866-68, letter to Pierre Fortin, Gaspé MP, Oct. 31, 1867; letter to John Hardeley, Nov. 1, 1867.
9   Ibid., letter to Robert V. Tancrête Winter of Douglastown, Oct. 2, 1867.
10   Ibid., letter to Pierre Fortin, Gaspé MP, Oct. 31, 1867.
11   For a description and maps of fishing banks in the Gaspé Bay see Roch Samson, "La pêche à Grande-Grave au début du XXe siècle," Histoire et archéologie No. 41 (1980) (hereafter cited as "La pêche"), pp. 34-41.
12   Fortin mentions that about twenty fishermen every year were caught in bad weather and killed. He adds that storms and strong winds often kept fishermen from going out for days or even weeks at a time. Rapports Fortin, 1859, p. 66.
13   PAC, MG 21, Add. MSS 21862, 1774-86, microfilm A-773. 1777 census report by Nicolas Cox.
14   Rapports Fortin, 1859, p. 49.
15   Ibid., pp. 65-66.

114

16 In 1856 and 1857 William Hyman paid ₤8.10 sterling for boats for his clients. PC, WHS, Ledgers, 1856-57, pp. 5, 7.

17 N. Cox, op. cit., p. 11.

18 David J. McDougall, "The Shipbuilders, Whalers and Master Mariners of Gaspé Bay in the Nineteen Century," in The Enterprising Canadians: Entrepreneurs and Economic Development in Eastern Canada, 1820-1914 (St. John's: Maritime History Group, Memorial University, 1979).

19 Rapports Fortin, 1862, pp. 82-85.

20 Roch Samson, "La pêche," p. 41ff.

21 Ibid., p. 98.

22 PC, ADH, Letterbooks, 1864-66, letter to John Hardeley, Mar. 7, 1866. Trawl fishing was for large fish (big cod) which were harder to market.

23 Rapport Têtu, 1868, p. 66.

24 Rapports Lavoie, 1874, p. 8.

25 Rapports Fortin, 1859, pp. 65-66.

26 Roch Samson, "La pêche," p. 94ff.

27 Rapports Fortin, 1859, p. 67.

28 Ibid., p. 68.

29 PC, ADH, loc. cit.

30 Ibid., Letterbooks, 1864-66, letter to Wade & Robson, Mar. 23, 1864.

31 Rapports Fortin, 1864, pp. 39-40.

32 Ibid., 1859, pp. 67-68.

33 Roch Samson, "La pêche," pp. 71-72.

34 Nicolas Denys, Description géographique et historique des costes de l'Amérique septentrionale.... (Paris: Claude Barbin, 1672), Vol. 2, Ch. 13, pp. 197-206; Henri-Louis duhamel du Monceau, Traité général des pesches.... (paris: Saillant & Nyon and Desaint, Vol. 2 1769), p. 92.

35 Charles de La Morandière, op. cit., Vol. 1, pp. 170-71.

36 Ibid., pp. 162-63.

37 See endnote 34.

38 Henri-Louis Duhamel du Monceau, op. cit., Vol. 2, pp. 89-90.

39 APC, MG 21, Add. MSS 21862, 1774-86, microfilm A-773; APC, MG 28, III, 18, Vol. 289 (Robin, Jones & Whitman Ltd. papers), Percé and Island of Bonaventure, list of fishing lots, 1784.

40 We are using the census-taker's territorial divisions. Although children's ages are not mentioned for Malbay, Percé or Bonaventure Island, they were included anyway. Thirteen Gaspé men out of sixty-six did not own boats, so they are not included in these calculations.

41 Roch Samson, "La pêche," p. 46.

42 Nérée Gingras, "Impressions de Gaspésie, en 1857," Le Canada-Français, Vol. 26, (Jan. 1939), pp. 492-93. Robin owned most of the southern cove at Percé. Thomas Pye, Images de la Gaspésie.... (Quebec: Editions Coméditex, 1980), p. 36.

43 Gazette de Québec, May 8, 1820.

44 Rapports Fortin, 1859, p. 67.

45 André Lepage, "Histoire de la population et du peuplement de la

péninsule de Forillon," Manuscript on file, Recherches historiques, Parks Canada, Quebec, 1978, pp. 32-33.

46 Marguerite Syvret, "Everyday Life on the Coast of Acadia and in the Province of Quebec, 1767-1787," Annual Bulletin of the Société Jersiaise, Vol. 21, Pt. 4 (1976), p. 471.

47 André Lepage, personal communication.

48 Roch Samson "La pêche," pp. 61-62.

49 PC, ADH, Letterbooks, 1864-66, letter to Z. Caron, Jan. 9, 1866.

50 Rapports Fortin, 1859: Fortin describes concisely how fishing was organized.

51 Rapports Fortin, 1856, p. 26.

52 Ibid., 1864, p. 9.

53 Ibid., 1859, pp. 51, 57.

54 Nérée Gingras, op. cit., pp. 490-92.

55 Thomas Pye, op. cit., pp. 36, 56.

56 See endnote 2.

57 Rapports Fortin, Têtu, Lavoie, Wakeham, 1862-1908.

58 Rapports Fortin, 1859, p. 65.

59 Nérée Gingras, op. cit., pp. 490, 496.

60 PC, ADH, Letterbooks, 1882-84, letter to F. Guilmet, Apr. 17, 1883: "Men's wages are very high, I prefer to have them here...." (translation).

61 In his Diary in 1869 (PC, ADH), Isaac Elias Hyman, William's eldest son, relates meeting Fabien Guilmet at L'Islet during a trip to Quebec in February. He refers to him as the company's principal recruiter.

62 In a letter from Hyman to Guilmet in 1880, the latter is identified as a bootmaker; he always recruited men for Hyman. PC, ADH, Letterbooks, 1877-80, letter to Fabien Guilmet, Feb. 9, 1880.

63 PC, ADH, Letterbooks, 1866-68, letter to C. Ouellette, Jan. 22, 1867.

64 Ibid., letter to Moïse Bélanger, Aug. 20, 1867.

65 André Lepage, "Le capitalisme marchand et la pêche à la morue en Gaspésie; la Charles Robin and Company dans la baie des Chaleurs (1820-1870)," PHD diss. in anthropology, Université Laval, 1983.

66 PC, ADH, Letterbooks, 1864-66, letter to A. Vautier, Oct. 24, 1864.

67 Ibid., in a letter to his Jersey broker, John Hardeley, dated Mar. 7, 1866, Hyman says that he already tried, unsuccessfully, to change his producers' method of salting.

69 Roch Samson, "La pêche."

70 See endnote 2.

III Production of Dried Cod: Social Aspects

1 PC, ADH, Letterbooks, 1864-66, letter to Smith & Cochrane, Montreal, Apr. 12, 1864.

2 According to M.H. Perley (Report on the Sea and River Fisheries of New Brunswick, 1852), the "trade price" was 20 percent more than the "cash price," and Gaspé merchants made about 25 percent profit on their yearly transactions with the fishermen (quoted in

Harold A. Innis, op. cit., p. 356, note 81). We did a few calculations from the fishermen's accounts, and found that the price
difference varied considerably from one product to another (our
example showed a rate of 35%) and that generally the rate of
conversion into "trade" on the fisherman's credit side was always
less than the rate applied to his debit. Conversion into trade was
always more profitable for the merchant.

3   Percé. Bureau du Protonotaire, record of notary A. Dumais,
commitment between fisherman C. Parent (and his minor son) with
Philippe Le Boutillier, Feb. 1, 1868, No. 65. Several commitments
pertaining to Percé are contained in this record.

4   PC, ADH, Letterbooks, 1864–1866, op. cit., letter to Têtu
& Garneau, July 26, 1865.

5   Ibid., Letterbooks, 1921-22, letter from Percy Hyman to Stanley
Hotton, May 4, 1921.

6   Roch Samson, "La pêche," p. 62.

7   Harold A. Innis, op. cit., p. 494.

8   Thérèse Savoie, op. cit.

9   James C. Faris, Cat Harbour: A Newfoundland Fishing Settlement
(St. John's: Memorial University of Newfoundland, 1973).

10 See especially Estellie Smith, Those Who Live from the Sea,
St. Paul, West Publishing, 1977.

11 Reports on the "Projet côte-nord," Département d'anthropologie,
Université Laval.

12 James C. Faris, op. cit., p. 117.

13 Ibid., p. 121.

14 See endnote 65, chapter two.

15 PC, ADH, Letterbooks, 1864-1866, letter to John Hardeley,
June 27, 1865, in which Hyman says he had to face a bad season,
but that he had made several engagements. The following fall, in a
letter to his Quebec broker, he admits his failure in these: "We all
burned our fingers with keeping draft boats this summer, I kept
twelve, and am sure I lost by them over £200, it is fortune of war,
we cannot always be making money." ibid., WHS, letter to Thomas
Fraser, 1 Nov. 1865.

16 PC, WHS, Ledger, 1868; several fishermen had salaries recorded in
their accounts that year.

IV   Fishermen in Debt

1   See David J. McDougall, op. cit.

2   Rapports Fortin, 1856, p. 12.

3   See chapter one.

4   Canada. Parks Canada. Archives of William Fruing and Company
Ltd., Clorydorme, 1904: Good Debts Paid, Bad Debts, Doubtful
Debts, Parks Canada, Grande-Grave Project, microfilm M-68.

5   Rapport Lavoie, 1872, p. 12.

6   Canada. Office of Agriculture and Statistics. Census Department,
Recensement de 1861.

7   Thérèse Savoie, op. cit.

8   For a preliminary study on the question, see André Lepage,
"Rapport de Travail: dossier propriété foncière, projet Grande-

Grave," Manuscript on file, Recherches historiques, Parks Canada, Quebec, 1979.

9   André Lepage has recently established the basis of such an approach to the study of the evolution and reproduction of domestic units in Chaleur Bay; see André Lepage, L'économie domestique des pêcheurs de la Baie des Chaleurs, clients de la compagnie Robin, 1826-1861, Ministère des Affaires Culturelles, Direction générale du patrimoine, Quebec, 1980.

10   Rapport Têtu, 1868, pp. 62-63.

11   Rapports Lavoie, 1872, p. 12.

12   J.-B.-A. Ferland, op. cit., pp. 410-11.

13   See Francis M. Gibaut, op. cit., p. 31.

14   Production advances were calculated as follows: means of production (salt, gear, rigging) plus payments made as salaries and credit notes to other individuals, plus cash debited to the fishermen-dealers.

Conclusion

1   See the many land transactions put through by the Hyman and Fruing companies in Appendix B. See also Roch Samson, "Gaspé."

2   In the exploitation of sugar plantations in the Caribbean, the credit system favoured by merchants and the financial assistance from 18th century London "factors" already conditioned commercial practices a century later in Gaspé: the two-price system (cash and credit), deduction at source of commissions by London factors, buyers, sellers a second time and bankers all at the same time. See Paul Butel, "L'apogée du grand commerce maritime" in Pierre Léon, ed., Histoire économique et sociale du monde, Paris: (Armand Colin, 1978), Vol. 3, pp. 88-92.

3   See Peter J. Usher, Fur Trade Posts of the Northwest Territories 1870-1970 (Ottawa: Northern Science Research Group, Department of Indian Affairs and Northern Development, 1971), and Alain Bernard, "La production marchande chez les Inuits de la rive sud du Détroit d'Hudson (1930-55)," MA Thesis, Université Laval, Quebec, 1977, which describes the role played by commercial capital in the economies of three Inuit groups in the New Quebec.

4   For a look at the socio-economic organization of haciendas and landed estates in Central and South America, see Jean Jacquart, "Tranditionalismes agricoles et tentatives d'adaptation" in Pierre Léon, ed., op. cit., Vol. 2, pp. 448-50 and Maurice Garden, "Les Amériques avant leur indépendance politique", In Pierre Léon, ed., op. cit., Vol. 3, pp. 245-55.

5   The establishment and expansion of Hyman's business gives an illustration of this, as does John Le Boutillier, mentioned in chapter one.

6   However, population growth favoured merchant capital because it allowed more goods to circulate. This growth was necessary for merchant capital, at least during the period when it was establishing itself in the area.

7   Table 1 shows a concentration of production around 1880 in the hands of four exporters, and **at the same time** a general drop in exports from the Port of Gaspé.

Appendix I
1   See Roch Samson, "Gaspé".
2   See works cited in endnote 1, "Introduction."
3   Martha Harnecker, Les concepts élémentaires du matérialisme historique (Brussels: Éd. Contradictions, 1974), p. 25.
4   Pierre-Philippe Rey, Les alliances de classes (Paris: Maspéro, 1973), p. 108.
5   Ibid., pp. 109, 111, 115.
6   Karl Marx, Le Capital (Paris: Editions Sociales, 1976), 1st book, sect. 3.
7   Ibid., Book 1, Sect. 1, Ch. 1: "Monnaie et marchandise."
8   I am using Marx's outline from Le Capital, Book 3, Sect. 4, Ch. 16: "Transformation du capital-marchandise et du capital-argent en capital commercial et en capital financier (capital marchand)."

SOURCES OF ILLUSTRATIONS, TABLES AND APPENDICES

Illustrations
3   PAC, loc. cit.
4   Ibid.
5   Ibid.
13   Rapports Fortin, Têtu, Lavoie, Wakeham, 1863-80.
14   PC, WHS, Ledgers, 1854-94.
22   Ibid., Ledgers, 1854-63.
23   Ibid.

Tables
1   PAC, RG 16, A2, Vol. 476, Ship registers outwards 1851-94.
2   Rapports Fortin, 1855-63.
3   PAC, MG 21, Add. MSS 21862, 1744-86, microfilm A-773, Census by N. Cox in 1777.
4   Rapports Fortin, Têtu, Lavoie, Wakeham, 1863-82.
5   Rapports Fortin, 1863-65.
6   PC, WHS, Ledgers, 1857-93.
7   Rapport Fortin, 1859.
8   Ibid., PC, WHS, Ledgers, 1860-61; Recensement de 1861.
9   PC, WHS, Ledgers, 1860-61.
10   Ibid., Recensement du Canada 1861.
11   PC, WHS, Ledgers, 1860-61; Canada. Recensement de 1861.
12   PC, WHS, Ledgers, 1854-63.
13   Ibid.; PAC, RG 16, A2, Vol. 476.
14   PC, WHS, Ledgers, 1854-63.
15   Ibid.
16   Ibid.
17   Ibid.

Appendices

A   Rapport Fortin, 1862, p. 107.
B   Thérèse Savoie, op. cit., Table 5.
C   PC, ADH, Letterbooks, 1864-66.
D   Ibid.
E   Ibid.
F   Ibid.
G   Ibid.
H   Rapport Fortin, 1859, pp. 66-67; Thomas Pye, op. cit., pp. vi and 55-60.

120

BIBLIOGRAPHY

Bernard, Alain
"La production marchande chez les Inuit de la rive sud du détroit d'Hudson (1930-55)", MA Thesis, Université Laval, Quebec, 1977.

Bernard, Antoine
La Gaspésie au soleil. Clercs de Saint-Viateur, Montreal, 1925.

Bérubé, Louis
"Une victime de l'âge de fer; le premier mouvement coopératif chez les pêcheurs de la Gaspésie." MA Thesis, Université Laval, Quebec, 1949. 2 vols.

Breton, Yvan
"The Introduction of Capitalism in Yucatecan Coastal Fishing." In B. Leons and F. Rothstein, New Directions in Political Economy: An Approach from Anthropology. Greenwood Press, Westport, Illinois, 1979. pp. 141-58.

Brochet, Aldo
"La pêche dans le golfe au XIXe siècle." Revue d'histoire et de traditions populaires de la Gaspésie, Vol. 15, No. 1 (Jan.-Mar. 1977), pp. 23-26.

Canada. Annual Report of the Gulf of St. Lawrence Fisheries Officer.
Appendices des journaux de l'assemblée législative de la Province du Canada pour les années 1854-1867: Rapports de Pierre Fortin.
Département de la marine et des pêcheries, Document de la session n° 12, 1868: Rapport de Théophile Têtu.
Département de la marine et des pêcheries, Documents de la session pour les années 1869-1879: Rapports de Napoléon Lavoie.
Département de la marine et des pêcheries, Documents de la session pour les années 1880-1914: Rapports de William Wakeham.

Canada. Office of Agriculture and Statistics. Census Department.
Recensement de 1861, comté de Gaspé.

Canada. Parks Canada. Quebec Region. Recherches historiques et archéologiques.
Archives of William Fruing and Company Ltd. Clorydorme 1904: Good Debts Paid, Bad Debts, Doubtful Debts, Grande-Grave Project, microfilm M-68.
Archives of William Hyman and Sons. Ledgers, 1854-1894 (incomplete), 22 books.
Private archives of David Hyman. Correspondence from Jersey Brokers, 1863-1887 (73 letters). Diary, 1869, I.E. Hyman. Letterbooks, 1864-1922 (incomplete), 9 books.

Canada. Public Archives.
MG 21, 862, Haldimand Papers, 1774-1786.
MG 28, III, 18, Vol. 289, Robin, Jones & Whitman Ltd. Papers.
RG 16, A2, Vol. 476, Ship registers outwards 1851-1894.

Chambers, Edward Thomas Davies
"Les pêcheries de la province de Québec: introduction historique," Contribution, n⁰ 1, Ministère de la Colonisation, des mines et des pêcheries, 1912.

Clarke, John M.
The Heart of Gaspé; Sketches in the Gulf of St-Lawrence. MacMillan, New York, 1913.

---. L'île Percée, the Finial of the St. Lawrence or Gaspé Flaneries, Being a Blend of Reveries and Realities; of History and Science; of Description and Narrative; as also a Signpost to the Traveler. Yale University Press, New Haven, 1923.

Denys, Nicolas
Description géographique et historique des costes de l'Amérique Septentrionale. Avec l'histoire naturelle du Païs. Claude Barbin, Paris, 1672. 2 vols.

Dictionary of Canadian Biography
University of Toronto Press, Toronto, 1982. Vol. 11: 1881-1890.

Duhamel du Monceau, Henri-Louis
Traité général des pesches et histoire des poissons qu'elles fournissent, tant pour la subsistance des hommes, que pour plusieurs autres usages qui ont rapport aux arts et au commerce, Saillant & Nyon et Desaint, Paris, 1769. 3 vols.

Faris, James C.
Cat Harbour: A Newfoundland Fishing Settlement. Institute of Social and Economic Research, Memorial University of Newfoundland, St. John's, 1972.

Ferland, J.-B.-A.
"Journal d'un voyage sur les côtes de la Gaspésie." Les soirées canadiennes (1861), pp. 301-476. Quebec.

Gazette de Québec
May 8, 1820.

Gazette des Campagnes (Sainte-Anne de la Pocatière)
1861-1872.

Gibaut, Francis M.
"Memories of a Gaspesian." Revue d'histoire de la Gaspésie, Vol. 1, No. 1 (Jan.-Mar. 1963), pp. 27-32. Gaspé.

Gingras, Nérée
"Impressions de Gaspésie, en 1857." Le Canada-Français, Vol. 26 (Jan. 1939), pp. 483-97. Quebec.

Hamelin, Jean and Yves Roby
Histoire économique du Québec 1851-1896. Fides, Montreal, 1971.

Harnecker, Martha
Les concepts élémentaires du matérialisme historique. Contradictions, Brussels, 1974.

Hart, Arthur Daniel, comp.
The Jew in Canada; A Complete Record of Canadian Jewry from the Days of the French Régime to the Present Time. Montreal, Jewish Publications, 1926.

Iffland, Dr. Anthony von
"Aperçu d'un voyage dans le district de Gaspé pendant les mois de mai, juin, juillet et une partie d'août 1821, par le Docteur von Iffland." Revue d'histoire de la Gaspésie, Vol. 7, No. 1 (Jan.-Mar. 1969), pp. 19-41, Gaspé.

Innis, Harold A.
The Cod Fisheries; The History of an International Economy, Rev. ed. University of Toronto Press, Toronto, 1978.

La Morandière, Charles de
Histoire de la pêche française de la morue dans l'Amérique septentrionale. Maisonneuve et Larose, Paris, 1962-66. 3 vols. Vols. 1-2: "Des origines à 1789"; Vol. 3: "De la Révolution à nos jours."

Lee, David
"La Gaspésie, 1760-1867." Lieux historiques canadiens: cahiers d'archéologie et d'histoire, No. 23 (1980), pp. 117-92. Ottawa. (Available in English as "Gaspé, 1760-1867," Canadian Historic Sites: Occasional Papers in Archaeology and History, No. 23, 1980, pp. 117-86, Ottawa.)

LeGros, Arthur G.
"Refutation of an Old Fantasy." Spec (Gaspé), Vol. 3, No. 8 (Oct. 24, 1977).

Léon, Pierre, ed.
Histoire économique et sociale du monde. Armand Colin, Paris, 1978. Vol. 2: 1580-1730; Vol. 3: 1730-1840.

Lepage, André
L'économie domestique des pêcheurs de la Baie des Chaleurs, clients de la compagnie Robin, 1826-1861. Ministère des Affaires culturelles, Direction générale du patrimoine, Quebec, 1980.
--- "Le capitalisme marchand et la pêche à la morue en Gaspésie; la Charles Robin and Company dans la baie des Chaleurs (1820-1870)," PHD diss., Département d'anthropologie, Université Laval, 1983.

---. "Histoire de la population et du peuplement de la péninsule de Forillon." Manuscript on file, Recherches historiques, Parks Canada, Quebec, 1978.

---. "Rapport de travail: dossier propriété foncière, projet Grande-Grave." Manuscript on file, Recherches historiques, Parks Canada, Quebec, 1979.

Marx, Karl
Le capital. Éditions Sociales, Paris, 1976. 3 vols.

McDougall, David J.
"The Shipbuilders, Whalers and Master Mariners of Gaspé Bay in the Nineteenth Century." In Eric W. Sager and Lewis R. Fisher, eds., The Enterprising Canadians: Entrepreneurs and Economic Development in Eastern Canada, 1820-1914. Memorial University, Maritime History Group, St. John's, Nfld., 1979, pp. 125-45.

Nadeau, Bernard and Pierre Provost
"Renovation of Historical Buildings." Spec (Gaspé), Vol. 3, No. 7 (Oct. 3, 1977).

Ouellet, Fernand
Histoire économique et sociale du Québec 1760-1850, Structures et conjoncture. Fides, Montreal, 1966.

Percé. Bureau d'enregistrement.
Registre A, Vol. 1 (1842-1849).
Registre B, Vols. 1-28 (1842-1919).
Volume 99, enregistrement No 47982 (1967).

Percé. Bureau du protonotaire.
Greffe du notaire A. Dumais.

Pouliot, J. Camille
La grande aventure de Jacques Cartier. N.p., Quebec, 1934.

Pye, Thomas
Images de la Gaspésie au XIXe siècle. Éditions Coméditex, Quebec, 1980. Reprint of 1866 ed.

Recherches sociographiques
"La basse côte nord du Saint-Laurent." Vol. 9, Nos 1-2 (1970), Quebec.

Rey, Pierre-Philippe
Les alliances de classes. Maspéro, Paris, 1973.

Roy, Charles-Eugène and Lucien Brault
Gaspé depuis Cartier. Au Moulin des Lettres, Quebec, 1934.

Samson, Roch
"Gaspé 1760-1830: l'action du capital marchand chez les pêcheurs,"

Anthropologie et sociétés, Vol. 5, No. 1 (Spring 1981), pp. 57-86. Quebec.

---. "La pêche à Grande-Grave au début du XXe siècle." Histoire et archéologie, No. 41 (1980), Ottawa. (Available in English as "Fishing at Grande-Grave in the Early 1900s," History and Archaeology, No. 41, 1980, Ottawa.)

Saunders, Arthur Charles
Jersey in the 18th and 19th Centuries. J.T. Bigwood, Jersey, Channel Islands, 1930.

Savoie, Thérèse
"Historique des établissements de pêche et compagnies du secteur de Grande-Grave." Manuscript on file, Recherches historiques, Parks Canada, Quebec, 1978.

Smith, Estellie
"Comments on the Heuristic Utility of Maritime Anthropology." Maritime Anthropologist, Vol. 1, No. 1 (Summer 1977), pp. 2-8. Greenville.
--- Those who Live from the Sea. West Publishing, St. Paul, Minn., 1977. American Ethnological Society, Monograph 62.

Syvret, Marguerite
"Everyday Life on the Coast of Acadia and in the Province of Quebec, 1767-1787." Annual Bulletin of the Société Jersiaise, Vol. 21, Pt. 4, 1976.

Université Laval. Département d'anthropologie.
"Projet côte-nord" reports.

Usher, Peter J.
Fur Trade Posts of the Northwest Territories, 1870-1970. Northern Science Research Group, Department of Indian Affairs and Northern Development, Ottawa, 1971.

Woodley, E. C.
"The Hymans of Gaspé." Revue d'histoire de la Gaspésie, Vol. 11, No. 2 (Apr.-June 1973), pp. 74-78. Gaspé.